CAREERS IN STARTING AND BUILDING FRANCHISES

By
CARLIENNE A. FRISCH

The Rosen Publishing Group, Inc.
NEW YORK

Published in 1999 by The Rosen Publishing Group, Inc.
29 East 21st Street, New York, NY 10010

First Edition

Library of Congress Cataloging-in-Publication Data

Frisch, Carlienne, 1944-
    Careers in starting and building franchises / by Carlienne A. Frisch.
        p. cm. — (Careers)
    Includes bibliographical references and index.
    Summary: Describes what franchises are and how they work, the education and training needed, different kinds of franchise businesses, career opportunities, and more.
    ISBN 0-8239-2781-4
    1. Franchises—United States—Juvenile literature.
  [1. Franchises—Vocational guidance. 2. Vocational guidance.]
  I. Title. II. Series: Careers (Rosen Publishing Group)
    HF5429.235.U5F75 1999
    381'. 13'0973—dc21   98-45097
                                     CIP
                                     AC

Cover photo © Archive Photography

Manufactured in the United States of America

About the Author

Carlienne Frisch is a freelance Minnesota writer who writes career biographies, business and travel articles, and historical pageants. Her non-fiction children's books cover such diverse topics as franchising, pet care, advertising, map reading, European countries, substance abuse, and author Maud Hart Lovelace. Frisch has B.S. and M.S. degrees from Minnesota State University-Mankato, where she is an adjunct mass communications instructor.

Acknowledgments

Robert Venneli
Jani-King of Seattle

Nikki Sells
Express Personnel Services
Springfield, Missouri

Arleen Goodman
Franchise Advisory Council
Brentwood, Tennessee

Karen Marshall
Computertots & Women's Franchise Network
Washington, D.C.

Barbara Weary
Mail Boxes, Etc.
Chicago

Elliot Eisman
McDonald's franchise owner
Owatonna, Minnesota

Don deBolt
International Franchise Association
Washington, D.C.

Susan Kezios
Women in Franchising
Chicago

Contents

SECTION III   LOOKING AHEAD

SECTION I

WHO, WHAT, WHEN, AND WHY

1

Welcome to Franchising: Introduction and History

When you hear the word *franchise*, you probably think of fast-food restaurants such as McDonald's, Hardee's, and Burger King. But franchising is more than burgers, fries, and shakes. From car repairs to computer maintenance, from pet care to home care, franchises are an important part of the United States economy. More than seventy industries have grown dramatically through franchising. There are more than 550,000 franchises in the United States alone, employing more than 8 million people, according to the International Franchise Association (IFA), based in Washington, DC. A new franchise business opens somewhere in the United States on an average of every eight minutes each business day. One out of every twelve business establishments is a franchised business. About one-third of franchise operations are *business format franchises,* or the kind of business most people think of when they think of franchising. (The various kinds of franchises are discussed in chapter 3.)

Franchising is a way of doing business. It is a method of marketing and distributing products or services. Franchising involves at least two kinds of people. The first is the *franchisor,* who owns the company and lends his or her trademark or trade name and business system to the second person. This second person, the *franchisee,* usually pays a one-time fee for the right to do business under the franchisor's name and system. The franchisee also pays a *royalty,* or percentage of sales, to the franchisor. The contract, or agreement, between the franchisor and franchisee is called a *franchise.* The term is also used to describe the business that the franchisee operates. For example, people say that a McDonald's restaurant is a franchise.

People from every walk of life purchase franchises. Opportunities are available for young people just out of college or other schools, for business and professional people seeking new jobs, and for retired people looking for another career.

Franchising is attractive because it offers opportunity to people with various levels of funding and experience. Young entrepreneurs and people with business experience are attracted to franchising because it gives them a chance to be independent and still work within an established system. Retired people find that franchises are a good way to remain active while earning retirement income.

If you are a self-starter, can work without supervision, get along well with people, can obtain financing, and are willing to follow a specific business system, buying a franchise may be the best way for you to get into business. The system is a key idea in franchising. Business format franchises offer you, the franchisee, a complete system for doing business as well as a well-known trademark and a logo. You pay for someone else's expertise, experience, and method of doing business. As the franchisee, you receive assistance in choosing an optimum location for the business, setting up the business, supplying product, training personnel, and marketing and advertising. Some franchises include a specific building design; like the *trademark* and logo, the familiarity of the building helps you market the product or service. When people see McDonald's Golden Arches, they know the food will be the same as it is at other McDonald's restaurants throughout the country. If they like McDonald's menu, they will stop to eat at a McDonald's restaurant wherever they are.

The public likes franchising because franchised businesses offer familiar names and dependable quality, but franchisors and investors also benefit. Selling franchises is a franchisor's best means of business growth. Investors have found that few financial investments can compete with the potential of a good franchise.

AN AMERICAN DREAM

It is not surprising that franchising began in the United States. Our nation's can-do spirit attracted immigrants from other countries, helped settle the American West, and created the industrial boom. That same spirit has led millions of would-be entrepreneurs to follow their dream of owning their own businesses. An *entrepreneur* is a person who organizes and directs a business undertaking, assuming the risk of possible financial loss in exchange for the opportunity of making a profit.

The word *franchise* means "to free." Franchising offers people the freedom to own, manage, and direct their own business. Each year, 20,000 to 25,000 people become franchisees. Let's look at how some franchises began.

For William Rosenberg, going into business for himself was a way to make money in an economy where many people were looking for jobs. In 1946, Rosenberg was one of millions of Americans looking for work. That year soldiers, sailors, marines, and airmen who had returned from service in World War II needed jobs. Instead of competing with them, Rosenberg found a niche selling sandwiches and coffee to factory workers from a truck. On the side of his truck he painted his business name: Industrial Luncheon Service. Three years later Rosenberg had 100 trucks in service. Because doughnuts accounted for 40 percent of his sales, Rosenberg decided to open a shop called Dunkin' Donuts. By 1955 he had sold some of his friends the right to open more Dunkin' Donuts shops, and a major franchise chain was under way.

Many other franchises grew in the post-World War II era. Colonel Harland Sanders went door to door, demonstrating a tasty chicken formula that became known as Kentucky Fried Chicken. Howard Johnson developed the restaurant chain that bears his name. Ray Kroc brought the McDonald brothers' burgers and fries to the entire country. His idea of franchising their fast-food service concept proved to be a success. (Chapter 2, "Welcome to McDonald's," describes the beginning and growth of McDonald's franchising and one franchisee's personal experience.)

FOUR DECADES OF FRANCHISING GROWTH

Many food franchises developed, as did many service businesses. In the 1960s, the franchising of Red Carpet Realty proved the advantage of wide-scale advertising and the training and referral of buyers and sellers nationwide. Following the same idea in the 1970s, Art Bartlett established Century 21, a successful nationwide real estate franchise. Century 21's brokers and agents have benefited from the trade name, the national advertising, and the nationwide referral network of buyers and sellers.

Although the recession of the mid-1970s caused hundreds of franchisors to fail and brought financial ruin to thousands of franchisees, especially in fast-food restaurants, the franchise method of doing business is sound.Franchising rebounded with the improvement of the national economy in the 1980s. Today almost sixty new franchise businesses go into operation every business day.

THE INTERNATIONAL FRANCHISE ASSOCIATION

In 1960 the International Franchise Association (IFA) was formed. It now has about 30,000 members, including franchisors, franchisees, the Council of Franchise Suppliers, educational institutions, and other franchise-related associations. IFA's mission is to enhance and safeguard the business environment for franchisees and franchisors worldwide. IFA serves as a resource center for current and prospective franchisees and franchisors, the media, and the government. The organization has helped develop legislation that safeguards franchising from abuse by fraudulent operators and supports programs that expand opportunities in franchising for women and minorities.

ABOUT THIS BOOK

The subsequent chapters of this book are designed to offer an in-depth explanation of the concepts of franchising and provide information you can use in deciding if franchising is for you. Section I discusses the "who, what, when, and why" of franchising, including what franchises are and how they work, guidelines for helping you decide whether you have the characteristics of a franchisee, the education and training needed, the advantages and risks of franchising, and its opportunities for women and minorities. Section II provides information on the "where" and "how" of franchising, including various kinds of franchises, how to get help in choosing and pursuing a franchise opportunity, how to finance one, and information on buying an existing operation. Section III looks ahead at franchising around the world and its market in the twenty-first century, including home-based franchise opportunities. In addition, the book includes a glossary of franchising and business terms, an appendix of organizations that offer franchising information and assistance, and a list of books and magazines that can provide further information on the subject.

2

Welcome to McDonald's: A Case History

The words "Welcome to McDonald's" are spoken in many languages around the world—30 million times a day, in 20,000 locations in 100 countries. When people think of franchises, McDonald's may be the first name that comes to mind. How did the international franchise get started? How did it grow so quickly? What's the secret of McDonald's success? The answers to these questions tell the story of a concept—fast food, low prices, and high quality standards—whose time had come. The growth of the concept depended on franchising.

A BURGER AND A DREAM

The McDonald's Corporation began with a little drive-in restaurant in San Bernardino, California, owned and operated by two brothers, Dick and Mac McDonald. In the years after World War II, their barbecue stand developed into a $200,000-a-year business, but the McDonald brothers wanted to improve it. So they phased out the carhops who carried orders to customers waiting in their cars and put in a self-service counter. They downsized a twenty-five-item menu to nine items: hamburgers, cheeseburgers, three soft-drink flavors, milk, coffee, potato chips, and pie. (French fries and milkshakes were soon added.) The brothers reengineered their stainless steel kitchen for assembly-line mass production.

When the McDonald brothers reopened their streamlined restaurant in December 1948, they cut the price of their hamburger in half, from 30 cents to 15 cents. By the mid-1950s they had annual revenues of $350,000, almost double the sales of their earlier carhop business. When news of their success was spread by a 1952 article in *American Restaurant Magazine*, they received up to 300 inquiries each month from interested entrepreneurs around the country. The McDonald brothers had a vision—other fast-food restaurants based on their successful operation in San Bernardino.

The first McDonald's franchisee was Neil Fox. The McDonald brothers designed Fox's restaurant in Phoenix, Arizona, as the prototype for the hamburger chain they planned to build. The red-and-white tiled building with a slanting roof had Golden Arches on the sides.

For as little as a thousand dollars, franchisees could receive the McDonald's name, a basic description of their Speedy Service System, and training from their original counterman, Art Bender. Still, the McDonald's franchising potential was barely being tapped until Ray Kroc came along.

Like many people of his generation, Kroc did not graduate from high school. After driving a Red Cross ambulance in World War I, he turned to sales work. He sold paper cups to sidewalk vendors in Chicago and real estate in Florida. By 1954, Kroc was a milk shake machine salesman who had built a good business as the exclusive distributor for "Multimixer." He visited his best customers, the McDonald brothers, who bought many milk shake machines from him. He hoped to discover how the McDonald brothers sold 20,000 milk shakes each month so he could help his other customers increase their sales volume—and buy more machines from him.

When Kroc arrived at the San Bernardino McDonald's and saw a fast-moving line of customers buying burgers and fries, he felt sure that people everywhere in the country would do the same. The brothers explained that, despite their vision, they had no desire to handle the expansion of their concept, so Kroc became McDonald's exclusive franchising agent for the entire United States. He formed the new franchising company on March 2, 1955, under the name of McDonald's System, Inc. A little hamburger-man figure called Speedee became the company's symbol.

In April 1955, Kroc's prototype McDonald's restaurant opened for business in Des Plaines, Illinois, a Chicago suburb. Art Bender, who had served the first McDonald brothers' hamburger, served the first hamburger at Ray Kroc's McDonald's. Bender went on to open the first of Kroc's McDonald's franchises in Fresno, California, and owned seven restaurants by the time he retired.

Fast, Friendly Service

Kroc's agreement with the McDonald brothers was to limit the franchise fee to $950 per restaurant and to charge a service fee, or royalty, of 1.9 percent of restaurant sales. Kroc added high cleanliness standards to the McDonald brothers' formula of a limited menu, quality food, assembly-line production, and fast, friendly service. Kroc also decided that the McDonald's system would not be involved in selling franchise owners their equipment, supplies, or food. The company did, however, purchase or lease much of the real estate on which the restaurants were located. Thus, if a franchise owner failed, so did Kroc.

Kroc used his sales skills to persuade franchisees to sign up, to line up prospective suppliers, to inspire the company's first team of managers, and to convince lenders to finance the company. Kroc believed so strongly in his vision that he drew no salary from the company until 1961. By the end of 1956 fourteen McDonald's restaurants had served 50 million hamburgers and had sales of $1.2 million. In 1960 McDonald's sold its 400-millionth hamburger and had 228 restaurants, reporting $37.6 million in sales.

To increase growth of the franchise, Kroc decided to buy out the McDonald brothers so he would no longer have to operate under their original agreement. The brothers asked for a flat $2.7 million in cash, of which they would pay $700,000 in taxes. This left $1 million for each of them, which they considered a fair price for inventing the fast-food industry. In 1961 Kroc obtained a loan to buy out the McDonald brothers. That same year he opened Hamburger University in the basement of a restaurant in Elk Grove Village, Illinois. There franchisees learned the principles of McDonald's management and customer service. Today McDonald's franchisees earn a degree in Hamburgerology from the new McDonald's Hamburger University, opened in 1983, at McDonald's headquarters in Oak Brook, Illinois.

The Golden Arches

In 1962 the Golden Arches officially replaced Speedee as the company's logo, and McDonald's advertising appeared nationally for the first time in *Life* magazine. The following year the Filet-O-Fish was the first new menu addition since the original menu had been created. Lou Groen, a McDonald's franchisee, developed the fish sandwich for "meatless Fridays" in the Roman Catholic neighborhood he served in Cincinnati, Ohio.

In 1965, to celebrate the tenth anniversary of Ray Kroc's opening of the McDonald's in Des Plaines, McDonald's stock was listed on the New York Stock

Exchange—an unusual achievement for a fast-food chain at that time. McDonald's stock sold for $22.50 a share. Anyone who bought 100 shares for $2,250 and held those shares for thirty years had 37,180 shares, worth more than $1.4 million. By April 1966 the stock had already split once, and investors had three shares for every two they had purchased.

In 1966 Ronald McDonald made his first national television appearance in Macy's Thanksgiving Day Parade. The following year the price of a McDonald's hamburger increased (from fifteen to eighteen cents) for the first time since the McDonald brothers opened their fast-food restaurant nearly twenty years earlier. Also that year the first international McDonald's restaurants opened in Canada and Puerto Rico, leading to formation of the International Division in 1969 and opening of McDonald's franchises in Japan, Germany, Australia, Guam, and Holland two years later. Today McDonald's restaurants operate in nearly 100 countries around the globe.

McDonald's success continued to reach new heights. A sandwich created by franchisee Jim Delligatti—the Big Mac—was added to the menu in 1968, along with the Hot Apple Pie. In 1969 McDonald's introduced Christmas gift certificates and a new building design, which employed the Golden Arches throughout. In 1970 a McDonald's restaurant in Waikiki, Hawaii, was the first to serve breakfast. A complete breakfast menu was added nationally in 1977, and by 1986 McDonald's served one of every four breakfasts eaten outside the home in the United States.

The first McDonald's Playland opened in Chula Vista, California, in 1971. The following years saw the Quarter Pounder, large fries, and Egg McMuffin (created by franchisee Herb Peterson) made available at the Golden Arches. Also in 1973, the first campus McDonald's opened at the University of Cincinnati.

The Ronald McDonald House

The following year McDonaldland Cookies were introduced and the first Ronald McDonald House opened in Philadelphia, Pennsylvania, to provide a "home away from home" for families of seriously ill children being treated at nearby hospitals. In 1984 Ronald McDonald House Charities was established, and a national fund drive raised $5 million. The first European Ronald McDonald House opened in Amsterdam, Holland, in 1985. Today, more than 165 Ronald McDonald Houses in twelve countries provide "homes away from home" for nearly 100,000 families each year. McDonald's and Ronald McDonald House Charities also make large disaster donations, such as nearly $1 million to victims of the 1995 earthquake in Kobe, Japan.

The Sky Is the Limit

The first drive-through McDonald's opened in Sierra Vista, Arizona, in 1975. Drive-through business now accounts for about half of McDonald's sales. Happy Meals were added to the national menu in 1979.

Kroc died in January 1984. By that time McDonald's had served 45 billion hamburgers, countless fries, shakes, breakfasts, and Filet-O-Fish sandwiches—and had added Chicken McNuggets to the menu. In 1985 Kroc's first McDonald's restaurant, in Des Plaines, Illinois, was restored to its original form and reopened as the McDonald's museum.

Fresh tossed salads were added to the McDonald's menu in 1987. That year clothing also was "added to the menu" when McDonald's granted Sears, Roebuck & Company the rights to carry a line of children's clothing called "McKids."

13

To address Americans' concern about fat in their diets, McDonald's introduced the McLean Deluxe sandwich in 1991, with a 91 percent fat-free beef patty. That year McDonald's also took to the skies when United Airlines began offering McDonald's Friendly Skies Meals to young passengers. The next year McDonald's food was offered in restaurant cars on the Swiss Federal Railroad. In 1993 McDonald's marked two new milestones. A McDonald's restaurant opened in a Wal-Mart store, and the first McDonald's-at-sea opened aboard the world's largest ferry, which transports vacationers across the Baltic Sea between Stockholm, Sweden, and Helsinki, Finland.

In 1995 the Fajita Chicken Salad was introduced in McDonald's restaurants throughout the United States—the same year that the first kosher McDonald's opened in Israel. Internationally McDonald's restaurants have standard menus but also offer foods that reflect a country's cultural preferences. In Arab countries McDonald's restaurants comply with Islamic laws for food preparation. Some McDonald's restaurants serve rice dishes and fried chicken in Japan, beer in Germany, kiwi burgers in New Zealand, salmon sandwiches, called "McLaks," in Norway, and the McHuevo (a hamburger with a poached egg on top) in Uruguay. In 1998 McDonald's responded to the Beanie Baby craze that swept the nation by including a Teenie Beanie Baby (made by Ty Company) in each Happy Meal.

The Franchisees
Nearly 4,500 franchisees and affiliates operate about 85 percent of McDonald's restaurants around the world. Franchisees in the United States must be individuals or families; McDonald's will not grant a franchise to corporations, business partnerships,

or absentee owners. (Internationally, however, McDonald's not only franchises to individual owners but also works with affiliates and with joint-venture partners.) Many individual McDonald's franchisees operate multi-restaurant businesses, with annual sales in the tens of millions of dollars.

Franchise owners contract to operate a specific McDonald's restaurant for a period of years, usually twenty, according to McDonald's standards of quality, service, cleanliness, and value. Many franchises are renewed beyond the original contract. McDonald's locates, develops, constructs, and owns the real estate, while the franchisee must equip the restaurant with kitchen equipment, lighting, signage, seating, and decor. The franchisee pays a one-time initial fee, an interest-free security deposit that is refundable at the end of the franchise term, a monthly fee based on the restaurant's sales, and a specified percentage of gross sales for marketing efforts. These include national and local advertising, promotion, and public relations. The franchisee's cost for buying a restaurant ranges from $408,600 to $647,000. A person may lease the operation for three years, make no payments, save the profits, and then exercise the option of buying the franchise.

McDonald's franchise owners can expect an extremely high success rate because they are carefully selected and thoroughly trained before they join the system. McDonald's franchise candidates agree to participate in about two years of part-time training and evaluation, which is designed to train them in all aspects of operating a McDonald's restaurant. Most of the training takes place in an operating restaurant convenient to their home. In addition, candidates receive three weeks of formal classroom sessions in regional training centers and two full weeks of seminars, conferences, and one-on-one sessions with corporate staffers at Hamburger University. Franchisees are expected to participate in the internal governing of the system, providing practical, grassroots viewpoints. For example, several franchisees have introduced menu items—Filet-O-Fish, Big Mac, and Egg McMuffin—which have become classics on McDonald's menus.

Elliott Eisman, McDonald's:

"From the time I was a kid, it was almost a legend—if you own a McDonald's, your life is made," Elliott Eisman says. "Now I know that's not so. It's a lot of hard work."

Elliott owns five McDonald's franchises in small towns in southern Minnesota. He is one of a small percentage of McDonald's franchisees who did not start out as either an employee or a supplier. Before beginning his McDonald's career, he worked for an accounting firm, and later in sales management for a steel company.

"When I worked in accounting, I saw the financial records of small businesses and I knew I wanted to run my own business someday," Elliott says. "I never even considered a different franchise. After seventeen years with the steel company, I opened my first McDonald's franchise in September 1989 in Minneapolis, Minnesota."

Without any McDonald's experience except as a customer, Elliott had to apply to be considered for a McDonald's franchise. He and his wife were interviewed for three hours at the corporate office in Oak Brook, where they both had to tell the story of their lives. Three weeks later, Elliott was told he had been accepted for a fifty-hour on-the-job evaluation.

"When I had worked the fifty hours, I had another three-hour interview," Elliott recalls. "I was told to learn the business by working twenty hours a week at a McDonald's, but not to quit my other job. McDonald's supplied a uniform and my food, but there wasn't any pay. I began working ten hours on Saturday and ten on Sunday. Although it could be done in one to two years, it took me three years to complete the training because the steel company moved me from Chicago to Kansas City. I trained in five different McDonald's."

Elliott's training also included textbook study alternating with hands-on courses in basic operations, intermediate operations, and equipment operation. He went through the same training McDonald's managers receive. The final phase of his training was two weeks at Hamburger University in Oak Brook. He paid his own lodging expenses and travel expenses from Kansas City.

"There's nothing we didn't do at Hamburger University," Elliott says. "We flipped burgers, plunged plugged-up toilets, and mopped up spills. I still do all of those things in my business. I didn't know the training would be as hard as it was. I think it is meant to weed out people who want it to be easy, because owning a McDonald's franchise is not magic. You get out what you put in."

After Elliott was approved for franchise ownership, the company told him about a franchise owner who wanted to sell one of his restaurants in Minneapolis because it was too far away from his other McDonald's. Elliott contacted the owner and negotiated the purchase of the contract, on which there were three years left. He raised $125,000 by cashing in his profit-sharing and retirement funds from the steel company, and he got a bank loan for $375,000. He rented the building with the Golden Arches from McDonald's (a company policy), received the right to use the name, signs, and equipment, and arranged the necessary insurance.

"I quit my job just before we opened, and we had a very lean first year," Elliott says. "We had three children, but we were able to take in enough income to rent a small house and pay household bills. I worked six or seven days a week, from 8 AM to 8 PM or later. We were open from 6 AM to 11 PM, so if my manager didn't show up, I would get a call from another employee around 5 AM, asking me to let him into the restaurant. It was hard to keep employees because it was an inner-city location. My wife would help out, too, and bring our baby to work with her. My record for days worked without a day off was twenty-one."

"We almost went broke with the Minneapolis restaurant," Elliott says. "Many customers would order just a hamburger and a glass of water. In 1991, I sold that restaurant and bought a McDonald's in Plymouth, Minnesota., where people have more money to spend. It was profitable. In 1995, I sold it, and took out a bank loan to buy a McDonald's restaurant in each of three small southern Minnesota towns. I added two *more in 1998. With five restaurants, our greatest challenge remains getting quality employees with a strong work ethic. If I could do any part of it over, I would delegate more responsibilities and hold people more accountable. Now, my managers are involved in the annual business plan and its goals."*

The Eismans train new employees with company materials and by pairing them with an experienced employee for several days. Their managers receive the same training Elliott had.

Elliott still works twelve hours a day, six days a week, but he spends less time flipping burgers than he did in Minneapolis. Each morning, he checks with his managers to learn who has an employee off and will need help during the lunch rush. He and his wife go their separate ways to wherever they are needed. After spending the afternoon at one of the restaurants, Elliott does paperwork in the evening. He also takes time to carry on a Ray Kroc tradition—volunteerism. Elliott volunteers in his community's Scouting program and with other organizations, and he serves on the Ronald McDonald House Board of Directors.

McDonald's employs 750,000 people, two-thirds of whom work in the United States. One-eighth of the current U.S. workforce has worked at a McDonald's at some time. Fred Turner, the Senior Chairman of the Board, started his career working in a McDonald's restaurant, and Ed Rensi, the current President and CEO of McDonald's USA, worked at the grill.

Today, McDonald's is one of the largest corporations in the world, generating sales of almost $30 billion a year. McDonald's is one of the key stocks that make up the Dow Jones Industrial Average. Every three hours, every day, a new McDonald's opens somewhere in the world. More than 12,000 restaurants are in the United States; 96 percent of the U.S. population has visited a McDonald's at least once, and 8 percent visit McDonald's on an average day.

3

Franchises: What They Are and How They Work

Franchising offers a small entrepreneur a good opportunity to compete with giant corporations that dominate a certain marketplace. Franchising offers you the freedom to own, manage, and direct your own business. By purchasing a franchise, you can sell goods and services that have instant name recognition in the marketplace. You can also obtain training and ongoing support to help you succeed. As with any freedom, there are responsibilities. In franchising, however, the responsibilities are clearly spelled out in a franchise agreement or contract.

TYPES OF FRANCHISES
There are three kinds of franchises: product and brand-name franchises, selected distribution franchises, and business format franchises.

Product Franchises
Product and brand-name franchising is often not recognized as a franchise method of licensing manufacturing processes. For example, most soft-drink bottlers are franchisees of Coca-Cola, Pepsi-Cola, or the 7-Up Bottling Company. The bottler buys syrups and products from the company and makes the soft drinks for local or regional distribution.

Selected Distribution

Selected distribution is such a well-established franchising method that most people do not recognize it as a formal franchise. It began as an independent sales relationship between a supplier, such as Ford Motor Company, and a dealer, such as Smith's Ford Sales and Service. The dealer concentrates on one company's product line (Ford cars and trucks) and identifies with that company. Gasoline service stations and appliance stores are other examples of selected distribution franchising.

Business Format Franchising

When people say "franchise," they usually mean business format franchising. That is the kind of franchising discussed in this book. In business format franchising, the franchisee purchases a complete system of doing business. The franchisee receives someone else's expertise, experience, and method of operation. The franchisor and franchisee have an ongoing business relationship. The franchisor provides a complete plan, or format, for managing and operating a business. The plan provides step-by-step procedures for all major aspects of the business, including a marketing strategy, operating manuals and standards, quality control, and ongoing guidance and assistance as well as the trademark and the product or service. The franchisor anticipates most management problems and provides a complete plan for management decisions the franchisee may have to make. The franchisee receives assistance with everything from personnel training to product supply, from site selection to advertising.

About 2,500 business format franchises exist in about seventy categories by type of industry. They include such diverse industries as restaurants, flower shops, real estate services, business services such as executive search firms, and many service businesses, such as video dating, cleaning, and windshield repair services. Business format franchises are expected to continue to increase, because the lifestyles of many Americans are creating a demand for more of the consistency in products and services that business format franchises deliver. More about the variety of business format franchises is discussed in chapter 8.

THE GROWTH OF FRANCHISING

As popular as franchising may seem, there are fewer than 6,000 active franchisors in the United States, with about 2,500 of those being in business format franchises. Yet, sales through franchised businesses have grown faster than the gross domestic product. The two advantages of franchising are that the business can be learned and that it usually works anywhere. The IFA lists more than seventy industry categories to describe its members. The mobile American consumer depends on and appreciates the consistent quality of franchised products and services. Wherever they go, people expect and want the same quality for their money, whether it's a hamburger, a motel bed, a lube job for their car, a security system, or a dating service.

The Start of a Franchise

How does a franchised chain begin? Imagine a store owned by an entrepreneur with a particular concept, like the McDonald brothers' Speedy Service System for hamburgers, shakes, etc. When a business is successful and growing, the owner may hire employees (as the McDonalds hired counterman Art Bender) and may even open a second restaurant or store and hire more employees. If the entrepreneur wants to expand without actually having to operate the additional locations, he or she may decide to franchise the business name and system to another entrepreneur—a franchisee—as the McDonald brothers did when they designed Neil Fox's business in Phoenix.

The Costs

In a franchise agreement, the franchisor sells a license to one or more franchisees. The license includes the basics that you, the franchisee, need to start the business. You receive the business plan and the name recognition of the franchise group. Other benefits include marketing strategies, advertising and promotion materials, inventory, training aids, advice on selecting a location, and a peer group of other franchisees. In return, you pay the franchisor an initial fee and, usually, monthly royalties. Under some contracts, you must also make a financial contribution to support national marketing and advertising campaigns. The franchisor may also have strict operating controls on your business, such as requiring you to purchase equipment and supplies from specific vendors. Some or all of the following fees may be written into the franchise contract.

Initial Franchise Fee and Other Expenses. The initial franchise fee, which may be nonrefundable, may cost from a few thousand to several hundred thousand dollars. As the franchisee, you may also incur substantial costs to rent, build, and equip a business location and to purchase initial inventory, such as carpet-cleaning machines and chemicals. The local, state, and federal governments may require operating licenses. Insurance is another cost. You may also be required to pay a grand-opening fee to the franchisor to promote the new business.

Continuing Royalty Payments. You may have to pay the franchisor royalties based on a percentage, usually 5 to

15 percent, of the weekly or monthly gross sales. Royalties must be paid even if the business does not earn significant income during the time period. In addition, under most contracts, royalties are paid for the right to use the franchisor's name. So, even if the franchisor fails to provide promised support services, you may still have to pay royalties for the duration of the franchise agreement.

Advertising Fees. You may have to pay into an advertising fund. Some portion of the advertising fees may go for national advertising or to attract new franchise owners, rather than to reach customers for your business.

The Controls
To ensure the uniformity that the consumer expects, franchisors usually control how franchisees conduct their businesses. The controls may put significant restrictions on your ability to exercise your own judgment. Five examples of controls are listed here.

Site Approval. To increase the likelihood that the new franchise business will attract customers, many franchisors must preapprove sites or locations for the business. They may not approve a site you prefer.

Design or Appearance Standards. Franchisors may impose design or appearance standards to make sure customers receive the same quality of goods and services at each franchise outlet. Some franchisors require seasonal design changes or even periodic remodeling and renovation. Complying with these standards may increase your operating costs.

Restrictions on Goods and Services Offered for Sale. Franchisors may closely restrict the goods and services you offer for sale. For example, if you own a restaurant franchise, you may not be able to add popular local menu items or delete items that are unpopular at your location. As the owner of an automobile transmission repair franchise, you may not be able to perform other types of automotive work, such as brake or electrical system repairs.

Restrictions of Method of Operation. Franchisors may require franchisees to operate in a specific way. The franchisor may require you to have your business open during certain hours, display only preapproved signs, provide employee uniforms, use certain advertisements, or even use certain accounting or bookkeeping procedures. These restrictions may prevent you from operating the business in the way you believe best. The franchisor may also require you to purchase supplies only from an approved supplier, even if you can obtain similar products elsewhere at a lower cost.

Restriction of Sales Area. Franchisors may limit your business to a specific territory. Territorial restrictions protect you from having the same franchise opened nearby and competing for the same customer base. The restrictions may keep you from moving your franchise operation to a more profitable location.

Terminations and Renewal
If you breach a franchise contract, you can lose the right to the franchise. In addition, the franchise contract is for a limited time, so there is no guarantee that you will be able to renew it.

Franchise Terminations. A franchisor can end the franchise agreement if, for example, you fail to pay royalties or fail to abide by performance standards and sales restrictions. If the franchise is terminated, you may lose your investment.

Renewals. Franchise agreements are typically made for fifteen to twenty years. After that time, a franchisor may choose not to renew the contract. In addition, a renewal may not provide the original terms and conditions of the agreement. The franchisor may raise the royalty payments or may impose new design standards and sales restrictions. The previous territory may be reduced, possibly resulting in more competition.

OPPORTUNITY VS. RISK
After reading this far in the chapter, you may have decided that franchising is too risky for you to consider. Do not give up yet. It is true there are risks in becoming a franchisee, but there are also opportunities. In chapters 9 and 11 are lists of questions to ask before buying a franchise or signing a contract. In addition, you can get advice from professionals, such as an accountant and an attorney, and from government agencies. There are also laws that apply to a franchisor's responsibilities.

The Federal Trade Commission Franchise Rule
The Federal Trade Commission (FTC) Franchise Rule is a U.S. government regulation that requires franchisors to prepare an extensive *disclosure document* and to give a copy to anyone who is interested in buying a franchise. The disclosure document includes more than twenty categories of information about the franchise: a complete description of the business, the type of experience required, the time and personal commitment necessary to run the business, the franchisor's track record and experience, the success rate of other franchisees, the cost of getting into the franchise, the cost

of the continuing right to operate the business, products or services the franchisee must buy from the franchisor, the terms and conditions under which the franchise relationship can be terminated or renewed, the number of franchisees who have left the system during the past few years, the financial condition of the company and its system, and franchise earnings claims. The franchisor should also provide you with a Uniform Franchise Offering Circular (UFOC) that contains information that will help you decide whether you are likely to make a success of the franchise opportunity.

4

Is Franchising for You?

You may be eager to own your own franchise operation. But, before that happens, you need to take several steps. First, you should evaluate your personality, abilities, and finances to decide if franchising suits you and if you are suited to franchising. You can do this by answering the questions in this chapter. Then, you need to examine various franchise industries, narrow your choices to a few franchises, investigate those franchises, and get full disclosure of information on them. You also need to prepare a business plan, get advice from an attorney and accountant, and talk with bankers and government loan agencies. You may also be able to involve the franchisor in helping you make financial arrangements.

GETTING TO KNOW YOU
Let's begin your personal evaluation by asking several important questions.

Are you willing and able to take on the responsibilities of managing your own business?
Any potential franchisee must make a self-evaluation before making what could be the biggest investment in his or her life. Franchise ownership is not easy. Although most franchisors will provide you with start-up training and ongoing support, you must be prepared

29

to manage the business. Some franchise operations may succeed under absentee ownership, but most require hands-on management. You must be willing to work harder than most people work at their full-time jobs. In a franchise, there is no such thing as a forty-hour work-week, especially in the start-up phase of the business. Workweeks of sixty to seventy hours are common. You must be willing to do whatever it takes, such as clean the grill, mop floors, stock shelves, empty the trash, handle an upset customer, keep the financial books, and discharge an employee who is not working out.

Jim Carollo is tired of punching the clock at an aircraft factory. He has also been taking business classes at a junior college, where he has learned that becoming self-employed is easier than it was in the past. National and state programs exist to help an entrepreneur begin and run a small business, including getting start-up capital. Technological developments have made running a business easier too. Computers, fax machines, and voice mail are all affordable for most small businesses.

Jim has also learned that the increasing popularity of franchises makes franchising a good opportunity for a person who wants to start a business but who wants to work with a proven idea. Jim wants to make more money, so he asked one of his teachers to help him decide about going into business. The teacher spoke with Jim about his goals and plans, his finances, and his family. These conversations helped Jim realize that he was in a good situation to start a business.

"There are many things a would-be entrepreneur should consider," Jim explains. "I work a lot of overtime

at the factory, so I know I have what it takes to put in the time I'll need for starting my own business. I'm not afraid of taking financial and career risks because I don't have a wife or kids, and my parents have always told me I can be successful at anything I try. My father started his own business when I was thirteen, and I used to go with him on some of his business calls. I've seen how hard he worked to become successful.

"I'm young and healthy, so I think I can go without the medical insurance that's a fringe benefit at my factory job," Jim says. "If I'm successful in my own business, I should be able to pay insurance premiums out of my own pocket. I think that would happen fairly soon, because I know I can make more money with my own business than I'm earning at the factory. I do enjoy my job, but it seems that I work harder than most of the other people there. My boss has complimented me for being reliable and honest, but I don't see any compliments in my paycheck. I don't think I'm being paid what I'm worth."

When Jim talked with the teacher, he learned a few things about himself. He realized that when he sets a goal, he doesn't give up, even though he may encounter difficulties and obstacles. Although he has many acquaintances and friends, his own satisfaction is more important to him than what other people think of him.

"I like making decisions about my work and being responsible for my own success or failure," he says. "I think I have a higher-than-average ability to get things done. Change doesn't bother me; in fact, I enjoy it when *something new happens. I can keep up a high energy level over a long period of time, and I have a strong sense of pride when I successfully complete a job or project. This means I'm well suited to being my own boss."*

Jim is right. He has the characteristics of an entrepreneur. He enjoys working hard, likes being independent and in control, wants financial success, and has a high energy level and a strong need to be successful. He also has self-confidence, determination, integrity, and a strong sense of personal responsibility for the results of his actions.

Jim's business education and experience are also assets. In addition, he grew up with a self-employed role model, his father, who can help him get business and legal advice and referrals from other professionals. Even without these connections, Jim could get help from SCORE, the Small Business Administration, and other resources that are discussed in chapter 10.

Will you enjoy the franchise?

Some people buy a specific franchise because they think it will make a lot of money for them. They find later that they do not enjoy the business. It is wise to buy a franchise that will be enjoyable and interesting to you for the next ten to fifteen years. Jim went to the public library and checked out several books on franchising. In the *Franchise Opportunities Guide,* published by the IFA, he looked through many pages of opportunities. The long list of various kinds of franchises impressed him. A list of franchise categories is given in chapter 8.

"I made a short list of those that sounded interesting, such as automotive work, cleaning and sanitation, security systems, and hardware and tools," Jim says. "This is the first step in deciding which franchises to consider. Then I read about franchises in each category. The books gave information on the franchise address, phone number, and contact person, how long the franchise had been around, a description of the operation, how much capital I would need to go into the business, the franchise and royalty fees, and what financial assistance and training were available."

Are you willing to follow the franchisor's system completely?
The key to franchising success is the consistency of product and service that customers find from one franchise to another. The sign and logo of a franchise—McDonald's Golden Arches, for example— indicate to customers that the franchisee is following a particular system.

People who are highly entrepreneurial do not like to conform to a predetermined formula and should be very careful about buying a franchise. People like Ray Kroc, who built the McDonald's empire, are the founders of franchises, not the franchisees. The founders have a vision and the overwhelming desire to make it come true. They usually believe they can do something better than anyone else, and they do not like rules or restrictions. They do not want to run their business according to someone else's rules. Anyone who possesses these characteristics is not likely to do well as a franchisee.

At first Jim was worried that he might be too independent minded to own a franchise. After he answered a series of questions in one of the books about franchising, however, he realized that he probably had the right kind of personality for it.

"I thought about how I like my work environment to be," Jim says. "I realized that even though I like being responsible and in control, I feel comfortable working in a structured, orderly environment. I can follow rules, so I would do fine working under certain controls."

While answering the questions, Jim thought about the pros and cons of being a franchisee as opposed to starting his own business. A franchise would limit his risk, make him part of a well-known organization, and provide a business plan and financing as well as management experience and assistance.

"Without more business experience, I don't believe I could start a business from the ground up," Jim explains. "I need more experience in marketing. A franchisor will help me with that business aspect. To make my business a success, I don't mind sharing my profits and being connected with a franchisor."

If Jim decides to become a franchisee, he will be expected to pay a franchise fee for a proven business operation, develop a long-term relationship with the franchisor, sell the franchisor's products rather than developing his own, and purchase goods and services according to directions from the franchisor.

Do you have a history of success in dealing with and interacting with people?

Many franchised businesses are based on people skills. A franchisee's ability to have a good relationship with the franchisor, other franchisees, employees, and customers is most important. A franchisor doesn't want a critical, negative franchisee who might give the entire system a bad name. A franchisee must have a track record of good relationships with employers, supervisors, and fellow employees.

"I wasn't the most popular kid in school, but I've always had quite a few friends," Jim says. "At the factory, the other employees don't seem to mind that our boss says I'm his best worker. Everyone is friendly during breaks and lunch, so I guess I have enough people skills to work with a franchisor, customers, and, eventually, employees."

Can you afford the franchise?

One of the major causes of business failure is under-capitalization. A franchisor can provide a good idea of start-up costs. The first step for the potential franchisee is a personal financial analysis.

When Jim decided he was strongly interested in purchasing a franchise, he knew he needed to prepare a financial analysis. Using guidelines he found in the books about franchises, he drew up three lists. The first list was a personal financial statement. Jim made two columns, the first for his personal assets, the second for personal liabilities. The list looked like this:

ASSETS		LIABILITIES	
Cash on hand	$231	Accounts payable	
Savings account	$500	(credit cards)	$447
Stocks or bonds	none	Loans payable	
		(auto)	$8,674
Loans receivable	none	Contracts payable	none
Accounts receivable	none	Real estate loans	$75,277
Real estate			
(home)	$110,000	Taxes	none
Life insurance	$5,000	Other liabilities	none
Automobiles	$8,000		
Other assets			
(furniture)	$5,000		

TOTAL ASSETS $128,731
TOTAL LIABILITIES $84,398
NET WORTH (Assets minus liabilities) $44,333

After Jim subtracted what he owes from what he owns, his personal financial analysis showed that he had $44,333 in net worth. Jim saw that some of that money is not liquid, or readily available for business use, but some of it is. If Jim goes into business, he can close his savings account, which he had earmarked for travel, and pay off his credit card debt, which he now pays in full each month with money from his paycheck. He will not sell his car (on which he owes more than its value) or his furniture, but he does have assets that provide start-up funds for a business.

Jim can take out a second mortgage on his home for a percentage of its net worth (which is more than $30,000), or he can sell the house and use some of the profit to buy a less expensive home with a smaller mortgage and lower monthly payments. He owes no taxes because his income tax is deducted from each paycheck, and the real estate tax on his home is included in his monthly mortgage payment.

Jim's other asset is his life insurance policy, which his parents took out when he was a child and which was fully paid seven years ago, on his eighteenth birthday. Because he has no dependents, Jim is willing to go without life insurance for a few years. He can cash in the policy or borrow the full $5,000 against the policy.

Jim's personal financial analysis shows that with his assets, he can raise $20,000 to $30,000 with which to start a business. He can consider buying a franchise that can be purchased and started for $25,000 or less. But a franchisee must have enough money not only to open the franchise, but also to run it until it is profitable. For some franchises, that may take a year. A banker or accountant can help you estimate start-up costs and monthly expenses.

5

Education and Training

Jim Carollo has taken business courses and has grown up with a father who was an entrepreneur, but some franchisees have little or no business education or experience when they purchase a franchise. If you fit this description, you should look for a franchisor who offers substantial training. This should include some business training as well as specific training for the franchise and about the franchised products or services.

ON-THE-JOB TRAINING

If you have experience managing or operating a small business, or if you have taken business courses at a college or university, you should still expect a franchisor to provide training in the franchise operation and product or service.

Some franchisees have experience in a particular industry, such as woodworking or restaurant work. If you choose a franchise in an industry where you have experience, you should look for franchise training that emphasizes the business aspects.

Nearly all franchisors provide some training, from a few days to several months. The training requirements and opportunities of each franchise are listed in books such as the IFA's *Franchise Opportunities Guide* and the *Franchise Opportunities Handbook*, written by LaVerne L. Ludden and based on information from the U.S. Department of Commerce.

For example, Pizza Pizza, Canada's leading pizza chain, provides a ten-week program that combines classroom and test-kitchen training with in-store practical experience. If you successfully complete the course, you should understand all aspects of operating and managing a Pizza Pizza outlet.

If you become a franchisee with Mail Boxes Etc., a packing and shipping service, you will receive two weeks of training at international headquarters in San Diego, California, and one week of training at the new Mail Boxes Etc. location. You will also receive ongoing support for marketing, operations, and communications. Mail Boxes Etc. also holds regular local, regional, and national conferences for its franchisees.

The Handyman Connection, a franchise that provides small to medium home repairs and remodeling services, provides two weeks of intensive training at its Cincinnati, Ohio, flagship operation. This is followed by one week with the franchisee when the operation is opened and further ongoing support.

EXPERIENCE REQUIRED

Some franchisors prefer that franchisees have general business experience or experience in the particular industry. These qualifications are listed for each franchise in the *Franchise Opportunities Guide*. The guide shows that if you want to purchase an Insty-Prints (business printing service) franchise, you will find sales, marketing, or management experience helpful, but not required. No printing experience is required because training in that area is provided. Many restaurant franchisors list a food service background as helpful but not required. Others, like Sbarro, Inc., require food service experience and the ability to develop the business location.

No Experience Required

Franchise opportunities are available for people who have no experience in a particular industry or a business background. Computertots, a company founded by former teacher Karen Marshall, is an example. It provides computer instruction for children. Although some computer skills are needed, they can be learned.

"You do not need a teaching or computer background," Marshall says. "We provide a week of training in Washington, DC. This includes the company's concept of education, marketing, how to teach classes to kids, and how to organize and manage a business, software, and computers. Sometimes we recommend that people get more computer training locally in their community."

Although Computertots does not provide any training at franchisees' business locations, you can e-mail or phone the company for support. The company also has a private bulletin board on the Internet so you can chat with other Computertot franchisees.

"It helps people to feel less alone," Marshall says. "It also brings issues out into the open, which is healthy. It helps us solve problems before they grow. It keeps all of us connected and learning."

Back to School

If you decide to take business courses before buying a franchise, you might study bookkeeping and accounting, computer technology, economics, finance, human resources (personnel), management, marketing, and business statistics. A college or university counselor can help you decide what classes will help you the most. Continuing-education classes are becoming more and more practical in their applicability to the workplace. These classes might be especially helpful to you as you further develop your skills and broaden your knowledge. If you have decided which franchise industries interest you, it will be easier for you to select the most appropriate classes.

6

Franchising Advantages and Risks

Franchising is a two-way opportunity. As a franchisee you get a proven way of doing business. The franchisor gets the opportunity to grow without the major capital expenditure required to form a non-franchised chain of restaurants, stores, or service businesses.

WILL YOUR FRANCHISE SURVIVE?

Statistics reflecting the success of franchises present differing pictures. Small Business Administration (SBA) statistics indicate that franchises have about a 62 percent success rate over a four-year period, compared with a 68 percent success rate for independent start-up businesses. Yet studies done by the U.S. Department of Commerce from 1971 to 1987 showed that less than 5 percent of franchise businesses closed up shop in any given year. In a study done at Wayne State University, Detroit, Michigan, 35 percent of the 1,300 businesses included in the study were out of business four to seven years later. In the same study retail franchises such as restaurants and shops had a mortality rate of nearly 50 percent. The study also showed that in the franchises that succeeded, the average profit was just $2,649, with the owner taking no salary for working sixty- to seventy-hour weeks.

John Reynolds, executive vice president of the IFA, says that certain studies put the failure rate at around

15 percent during a franchise's first five years. Reynolds says that franchises have a better chance of success than independent business start-ups for two reasons. First is the evaluation process you go through before buying into a franchise opportunity. Second, the business structure and support you receive increase the likelihood that your business will be successful.

Buying into a franchise has both positive and negative aspects—advantages and risks. The advantages include the experience of the franchisor, assistance in financing, a turnkey operation, training that is provided by most franchisors, use of the franchisor's buying power and advertising clout, the franchisor's ongoing advice, research, and development, and business synergy. The risks include a binding contract, working within the system, the entrepreneurial risk, a long-term working relationship with the franchisor, false expectations, and the actual management of the business.

THE ADVANTAGES

The Experience of the Franchisor

When you buy a franchise, you purchase the proven methods and years of experience of the franchisor. In many new businesses much time and money are spent in trial and error. A proven franchise system, along with adequate training, will reduce or eliminate many of your start-up problems. This means that you can open a franchise business with little or no previous experience in a particular industry.

Assistance in Financing

Some franchisors provide assistance in financing. The franchisor may make arrangements with a bank or other lending institution to lend you money. You must accept personal responsibility for the loan, but the franchisor's involvement usually increases the likelihood that the loan will be approved.

A Turnkey Operation

Many franchises offer turnkey operations, which means that the business name, operating procedures, trademarks, and patents are ready for you to use. All you have to do is to turn the key and begin doing business. This is an advantage for entrepreneurs who may not be sure what equipment they need, how much inventory they should buy, and what products and services are in demand where they are starting the business.

Training

As mentioned in chapter 5, many franchisors provide training for new franchisees. This usually takes place both at the franchisor's home office and at the franchisee's place of business. The training should prepare you in all facets of the business.

Buying and Advertising

Although most small-business people cannot afford to buy inventory products in bulk or to do extensive advertising, you buy this advantage with the purchase of the franchise. You have the right to use the franchisor's purchasing power and advertising. Most franchisors provide advertising advice and help. A major advantage is the American public's increasing awareness of franchises. As families travel, many look for McDonald's Golden Arches, the Perkins Family Restaurants' signs, a Bonanza Restaurant, or the symbol of their favorite franchise restaurant.

Advice, Research, and Development

Even after your franchise operation is open, you will continue to need assistance throughout the entire time you operate the business. The franchisor's staff of experts can help you in all aspects of your business. The franchisor may also provide ongoing research and development, including new products and services you can add to the business operation.

Business Synergy

The word *synergy* refers to the idea that the sum of the whole is greater than the separate parts. This principle can be applied to franchising. The idea is that through the support and assistance of the franchise organization, all franchisees will become successful. They become part of a "family" in which all members work together for the good of the whole. Often some of the best ideas for improving or growing the franchise operation come from franchisees.

THE RISKS

A Binding Contract

When you buy a franchise, you sign an agreement with the franchisor that you will follow certain guidelines as to how the franchise will be operated, the fees you must pay, etc. If you later have problems with the franchisor, you are still legally bound to follow the rules set out in the agreement. If you buy a franchise, you should go into it with your eyes wide open.

Working Within the System

As mentioned in chapter 4, following the franchisor's system is absolutely critical, because customers expect the restaurant, business service, or remodeling service to be the same everywhere. If you have difficulty following directions or dislike working within a system, you will find franchising very frustrating. But some franchise systems have areas, such as marketing, in which you can be creative. It is important to make sure you can work within the rules and regulations set out in the franchise agreement.

Entrepreneurial Risk

Part of your risk as a franchisee is that the franchisor will go out of business. Some franchisors are undercapitalized and do not have the ability to fulfill their own plan and projections. A financial advisor or accountant can help you reduce your risk by examining the franchisor's financial information.

Part of your entrepreneurial risk is you. If you buy a franchise that offers national name recognition, a system that is tested and successful, and excellent training, will this guarantee the success of your business? No! You will be the one who determines the success of your business. Motivation, the willingness to work hard, good judgment—these and other characteristics mentioned in chapter 4—will make the difference between your success and failure.

"Marriage" to the Franchisor

Buying a franchise is similar to getting married. Both are legally binding relationships that are meant to last for a long time. Your relationship with the franchisor and the franchisor's staff is extremely important. Before purchasing a franchise, you should visit corporate headquarters, pick up vibes and get a feel for the staff, and see if the operation seems to run smoothly. You should also talk with current franchisees about their relationship with the franchisor and try to read as much about the franchise as possible.

False Expectations

You may know the owner of a franchise operation that has been extremely successful. This should not lead you to expect instant success as a franchisee. Like any other business, franchising requires much time, initiative, and hard work. By talking with franchisees and the franchisor, you should get a realistic picture of what the franchise operation requires.

Managing the Business
Business experience or training and the ability to get along with people are both important in managing a franchise. You must honestly assess your preparation and ability to run a business and to seek assistance and advice in the areas where you need it.

FRANCHISING AND THE LAW
Franchising is an exacting and time-consuming process, with certain required procedures and restrictions, but this does not eliminate all risk for you. In 1979, the FTC issued a rule called the Federal Trade Commission Franchise Rule. It requires a franchisor to provide you with a written disclosure of certain information. Some states require the franchisor to register or file the disclosure. This written document must be given to you at least ten business days before the execution of any agreement or the receipt of any money by the franchisor. The disclosure document has twenty-three categories of information about the franchise. These include a complete description of the business, the hours and personal commitment necessary to run the business, the franchisor's track record, the business experience of officers and directors of the company, the basic investment to get into the business, the required fees for the right to operate the business, the bankruptcy and litigation history of the company, the term of the franchise, a financial statement of the franchisor, earnings claims (if the company makes them), the products and services the franchisor requires the

franchisee to purchase, the number of franchisees that have left the system in the past few years, the type of experience required in the franchised business, and other information.

Even with this, you have no guarantee that the franchise is of any value or that the information submitted by the franchisor is true. If the information is not true, however, the franchisor is subject to civil and criminal lawsuits.

Some businesses try to avoid revealing the required information by calling their business endeavors partnerships. This does not mean that all partnerships are franchises or that they are illegal. But if you enter into a partnership with a con artist, your major risk is that the selling partner does not have capital and does not want to reveal the information that would be required if the business were a franchise. One way to avoid such problems is to consider only franchises listed in reliable publications, such as the IFA's *Franchise Opportunities Guide*. Companies that belong to the IFA must meet certain membership requirements. They must have a satisfactory financial rating, comply with applicable franchise laws, and agree to follow certain standards of business conduct and practice.

The IFA recommends that you have an attorney examine a franchise agreement before you sign it. It is important to work with an attorney who understands franchising, especially antitrust law, trademark law, the FTC Franchise Rule, and applicable state law. In addition, you should have an accountant examine the terms of the franchise agreement and the franchise *prospectus,* or offering.

There are other publications you may find useful. To obtain a copy of the free FTC publication *A Consumer Guide to Buying a Franchise,* call 202-326-2222. The IFA has a guide entitled *Investigate Before Investing.*

Mediation

What if you have a problem or a dispute with the franchisor after the agreement is signed? You can get help through the National Franchise Mediation Program (NFMP), but franchisors are not required to let you know about it. The NFMP is a voluntary and informal process by which franchisees and franchisors can resolve differences.

To begin the mediation process, you must send a Dispute Letter to the franchisor. A copy of the letter should also be sent to the Center for Public Resources, Inc. (CPR), a nonprofit organization that specializes in mediation processes and is the organization behind the NFMP. When a franchisor receives a Dispute Letter, he or she must participate in the mediation process. If you receive a Dispute Letter from the franchisor, you do not have the same obligation. If you and the franchisor agree to work toward a resolution, you must meet and work toward it together. If CPR is not notified that the dispute has been successfully resolved, it selects possible mediators from your franchise region. You and the franchisor must jointly choose a mediator from among them. You share the cost of having the mediator. The mediator cannot force a solution on either of you but is there to help negotiate solutions to your problem.

The NFMP is a completely confidential process that is usually completed quickly and at moderate cost. A franchisor who participates in the program must make a two-year commitment to it. For free information about NFMP, contact the IFA Government Relations Department at (202) 628-8000.

7

Opportunities for Women and Minorities

Does franchising offer women and minorities an opportunity to sit in the front row of the business world? The answer depends on whom you ask.

The U.S. Department of Commerce stopped tracking franchise statistics in 1986. In its 1986 survey of 2,177 franchise companies, the Department reported that 26 percent of a total of 10,142 franchise units were owned by minorities. Of those franchise units, 3,615 were owned by African Americans, 2,808 by people with a Hispanic surname, 3,616 by Asian Americans, and 103 by Native Americans.

In the 1990s, the face of franchising remained white and male, according to Susan P. Kezios, the founder of Women in Franchising (WIF), an organization that provides franchise consulting services for women and minorities who are interested in becoming either a franchisee or a franchisor. WIF's surveys of franchising companies seven years apart—in 1987 and 1994—showed no increase in the percentage of women and minorities owning franchises. Results of both surveys showed 11 percent of the franchise operations were owned by women and another 20 percent were owned by at least one man and one woman together.

Another organization, the National Foundation for Women Business Owners, sees a different picture. The foundation predicts that by the year 2000, half of all businesses will be owned by women and African American, Asian, and Hispanic women will account for the majority of the growth in numbers.

Recent statistics on minority and women's ownership of franchises do not exist. Neither franchisors nor government agencies keep such statistics. In 1998, WIF was in the process of conducting a survey for the U.S. Small Business Administration, with results to be available in 1999.

Even without statistics, franchising leaders believe that a majority of the operations owned by minorities are in some of the most popular franchising industries. These include restaurants, automotive products and services, food retailing, convenience stores, and business services.

DIVERSITY IS AN ADVANTAGE

Franchising offers one major advantage to a woman or a person of color who wants to start a business—a way to obtain financing. Borrowing money to open a business is a challenge to any new entrepreneur. It has always been even more of a challenge to women and minorities because they often do not have a business background, a substantial credit record, and the collateral a lender requires. Franchising should provide a way around these obstacles, because franchisors recognize an increasing need to help franchisees find start-up funds. Because franchisors need franchisees for business growth, you should expect a franchisor to help you plan how to get financing. A franchisor may also help you obtain loans from the SBA, local banks, or private investors; arrange for property leases; and in some cases take part in your business venture by providing financing for equipment purchases.

But the reality of the situation may be different from the ideal. Kezios says that many women and minorities still hit a "glass ceiling." This refers to the problem women face when they reach a certain level of responsibility, pay, and power and then run into an invisible "glass ceiling" that bars them from going higher. Women and minorities may find that a franchisor does not return their calls about the company's disclosure document, and that even when they have a good business plan, they have difficulty getting bankers to take them seriously. Minorities may find their growth potential limited. One example Kezios gives is that Asian Americans who want to operate a franchise in the lodging industry find they are limited to owning budget lodging franchises.

Let's look at the franchising experiences of two women. One, Barbara Weary, is African American.

She Did Her Homework

Barbara Weary, Mail Boxes Etc.

Since 1996 Barbara Weary has owned and operated a Mail Boxes Etc. franchise in a predominantly white area of Chicago. As a middle-aged African American woman she had a positive experience in choosing a franchise, but she had difficulty getting financing despite her business education, a corporate business background, a good financial situation, and a solid business plan.

"I had 25 years of work experience in business and a Master of Business Administration (MBA) degree with a focus in finance and human resources," Barbara says. "But I had to jump through hoops that most other

people don't have to jump through. For example, I had to provide three months of security deposit on the business property lease, even though other franchisees had to put up only two months."

Barbara's business background and education both included finance and customer service (which is critical in a retail business like Mail Boxes Etc.). She had worked as a bank employee for thirteen years and then held an upper-management position in the human resources (personnel) department of a newspaper company. There, she taught customer service skills to other employees.

"I was a widow and wanted to go into business for myself, so I did my homework," Barbara says. "I analyzed my own interests. I went to franchise conventions. I decided I wouldn't open a business I didn't like because I knew I would spend my time working in it. I knew I had limited funds, liked working with people and was good at it, would need support and training, definitely did not want food service, and did not want to take five years to build my business. Because I was over fifty, I wanted something I could get into, learn fast, and begin making a profit."

After investigating a number of companies, Barbara decided Mail Boxes Etc. came close to matching her list of wants and needs. The master franchisor, who represented the franchise company, stayed in frequent contact with her. Without pressuring her, he provided information such as a list of all Mail Boxes Etc. franchisees in the Chicago area.

With her finance background and with assistance from Samuel Crawford of the American Franchisee Association in Chicago, Barbara took a year to draw up a business plan. After cashing in stocks and other financial assets she had built up over the years, she had $70,000 to put toward the business, which was $20,000 more than the cash requirement of $50,000. Barbara also met the net worth requirement of $150,000 with the value of her condominium and a pension fund she had not cashed in. The total investment needed for a Mail Boxes Etc. franchise outlet is $109,000 to $164,000. Barbara believed she was in a good financial situation to get the loan she needed. The first two banks she approached turned her down, including one bank known for being friendly to minorities.

"No one said I didn't have a good business plan," Barbara says. "I was committed to putting my life savings into the business. They just didn't listen to my passion and desire to do this. Both times I was turned down by women. In one phone interview, the woman said I didn't sound like I would be successful."

Barbara believes her age was probably not a factor in the discrimination she encountered. She believes that other people her age who had lost their jobs when corporations downsized their staffs and were also looking for business opportunities, did not have the same problems she did. Barbara believes being an African American was a more important factor than her age or gender.

Eventually, with Crawford's help, Barbara got an SBA loan and bought her franchise. She completed two weeks of franchise training in California, from 7 AM to 5 PM each day, and says, "As a former corporate trainer, I was impressed." This was followed by a week of on-the-job training in a Mail Boxes Etc. franchise outlet.

"We also have step-by-step manuals for every function, because this is a paper-intensive and detail-oriented business," Barbara says. "As soon as I was trained, I opened for business. The company provides local as well as national advertising, but to build my business quickly I handed out advertising flyers on street corners and contacted the managers of local businesses and high-rise buildings. I began making a profit in twelve to eighteen months." Until then, Barbara lived on some of the money she had saved. Four years after opening, she had three employees, one of whom is her son, who will eventually own the business. Barbara plans to add two more Mail Boxes Etc. outlets to her enterprise.

"I work sixty hours a week over five days, but I love it because it's mine," she says. "About 80 percent of my customers are white. My advice to anyone who is having a problem getting financing is to do your homework, prepare a good business plan, and be persistent. Someone will take a chance on you."

A Woman with a View

Arlene Goodman, Kampgrounds of America, Inc. (KOA)

Arlene Goodman had a ringside seat from which she watched a successful franchise operation and was able to buy into it. In 1976, she began working as a tour guide in Nashville, Tennessee, for a group of partners who also owned the Kampgrounds of America franchise in Nashville. Arleen decided she should be in business for herself when she found herself working on a day she wanted to spend with her family.

"I worked on Mother's Day so another woman could have the day off," Arleen says. "I had a three-year-old at home and wanted to be there. That's when I decided that I might as well have my own business someday, and have people work for me on holidays."

Arleen compared the KOA franchise contract with several others and liked the idea that it was simple compared to the other contracts. She was sure she could succeed as a KOA franchisee because she had met successful female franchisees. Tourism is the second largest industry in Tennessee, and she knew KOA was a well-established company. Its franchises have been sold since 1962, one year after the company was formed.

In 1982, Arleen got her chance when one of the partners decided to sell out. Arleen sold her house and bought into the KOA franchise with $18,000 she received from the sale of her house. She owned 5 percent of the franchise. Most of the franchise was owned by a large corporation. When the corporation wanted to sell off its investments, the partners got a bank loan to buy out the corporation in 1993.

"It was very rewarding for me and my partner (a man) to walk into a bank and have the banker say,

55

'Yes, I will lend you 2 million dollars,'" Arleen says. "Bankers look for collateral, whether you're male or female. My percentage of the business had been providing profits."

Because Arleen was familiar with the KOA franchise system, she did not take part in the training program, but she attends KOA seminars for updates. She has also founded other small businesses, all related to tourism, such as management services for a transportation company.

"I spend about 75 percent of my time on my KOA franchise, year-round," Arleen says. "I've worked many days from 6 AM to 1 AM. We have a staff of eighty, but sometimes I'm the person who calls someone to fix a toilet. The campground, which has 460 sites, including twenty-five cabins, makes a profit only 120 days of the year, but I have a consistent 20 percent return on my investment before taxes. The rest of the year we have income, but expenses exceed it. We make capital improvements, train employees, etc."

Arleen believes that franchising opened many doors for her. She was one of the founding members of the American Franchisee Association and was the first woman to be elected president of the International KOA Owners Association. When IFA opened its membership to franchisees in 1993, she was one of the first to join, and she served on the Franchisee Advisory Council. Nashville Life magazine chose her as one of the twenty-five most influential women in Nashville. She has also worked as a registered lobbyist for tourism.

"Being in business while my daughter was growing up made me a good role model," Arleen says. "In franchising, we don't even think about people's reaction to our being women. We're just out there doing the job, but franchising does provide us with instant credibility and acceptance by leaders in the Chamber of Commerce and other business circles.

"Many franchise companies have departments for recruiting women and minorities, and then they provide great support," Arleen says. "My advice to women is to do your homework, develop your relationship with a bank before you need financing, and make sure you understand the franchise contract before signing it."

"No Glass Ceilings"

A woman who is considering the purchase of a franchise opportunity may want to give particular attention to franchise companies founded by women. Karen Marshall, the founder and president of Computertots, has three times as many women franchisees as men. She also chairs the IFA's Women's Franchise Network, whose slogan is "No glass ceilings."

"About 70 to 75 percent of Computertots franchisees are women," Marshall says. "Ten percent represent minorities—Hispanics, African Americans, and Asian Americans."

Marshall is a former teacher who left the classroom when her child was born and founded Computertots in 1984. The business, which provides computer instruction for children ages three through twelve in schools and day-care centers, has been franchised since 1989. In 1998, there were 120 Computertots franchisees in the United States and an equal number in other countries.

To contact Marshall about women's opportunities in franchising, write to her at Computertots, ECW Corporation, 10132 Colvin Run Road, Great Falls, VA 22066, phone 703-759-2556, or fax 703-759-7411.

SECTION II

WHERE AND HOW

8

Types of Franchises

Thousands of franchise opportunities are listed by industry category in books such as *Franchise Opportunities Handbook* and the IFA's *Franchise Opportunities Guide*. Each franchise entry includes the company name and contact information, a brief description of the business, the number of franchisees, the year the franchise was established, the equity capital a franchisee must have, financial assistance available, and training and management assistance provided. You can use such guides to consider many kinds of franchise opportunities and then to contact the franchise companies that interest you for additional information.

At the end of this chapter is a list of franchise industry categories. For six of these categories, complete information is given about two franchises in each industry. This is the information you can expect to find in franchise opportunity guides.

ACCOUNTING/TAX SERVICES

Triple Check Income Tax Service, Inc.
727 South Main Street
Burbank, CA 91506
Ph: 818-840-9077
Fax: 818-840-9309

Contact: David Lieberman, President

Type of Business: Income tax service. Business service and financial service.

History: In business since 1970; franchising since 1977; 300 franchised units and one company-owned unit.

Cash Investment: $5,000 to $15,000 start-up. Indirect financing available. Company may act as guarantor for loans from commercial bank for payment of annual fee.

Training and Support: Eighty hours of training each year; advanced tax preparation training.

Qualifications: Owner of existing income tax and accounting business with a minimum of 100 clients, or $5,000 to $15,000.

International: Europe

E.K. Williams & Company (The Dwyer Group)
1020 North University Parks Drive
P.O. Box 3146
Waco, TX 76707
Ph: 800-992-0706 or 817-745-2424
Fax: 817-745-2566

Contact: David Bethea, Executive Vice President, or Gale Dudley, Regional Vice President

Type of Business: Accounting, counseling, and tax service to business owners.

History: In business since 1935; franchising since 1947; 200 franchised units.

Cash Investment: $40,000 to $50,000 start-up cash; $65,000 to $75,000 total investment.

Training and Support: Initial two-week training in Waco; follow-up consisting of three on-the-job training days, and eight training meetings per year. The first year has a fifty-week training cycle.

Qualifications: Background in accounting or book-keeping desirable. A strong desire to work with and counsel business owners.

ADVERTISING/DIRECT MAIL SERVICES

Money-Mailer, Inc.
14271 Corporate Drive
Garden Grove, CA 92643
Ph: 800-596-2453 or 714-265-4100
Fax: 714-265-4091

Contact: Franchise Sales Department

Type of Business: Cooperative direct mail advertising.

History: In business since 1979; franchising since 1980; 651 franchised units.

Cash Investment: $15,000 to $22,000 start-up cash. Financing assistance available.

Training and Support: Five weeks of classroom and field training for regional owners. Local franchisees receive mandatory two-week training (one classroom, one in field).

Qualifications: For franchise program, individuals with sales/marketing experience. For regional program, individuals with proven sales/marketing management background.

The Homesteader (Homesteader Enterprises)
P.O. Box 2824
Framingham, MA 01703
Ph: 800-941-9907 or 508-820-4311
Fax: 508-820-0280

Contact: Allen Nitschelm, President; Judy Cader, Vice President

Type of Business: Publishes direct-mail pieces, sends to target market of new homeowners.

History: In business since 1989; franchising since 1993; twelve franchised units, six company-owned units.

Cash Investment: $4,000 to $8,000 start-up cash. Total investment of $7,000 to $22,000. Franchise fee of $5,000 payable in two installments over six months.

Training and Support: Extensive operations manual, two days of classroom training, one day field training, and free telephone consultations.

Qualifications: Experience or strong interest in sales. Computer, writing, or business experience helpful.

ART SUPPLIES

Kennedy Studios
140 Tremont Street
Boston, MA 02111
Ph: 800-448-0027 or 617-542-0868
Fax: 617-695-0957

Contact: Kevin G. Richard, General Manager

Type of Business: Art and framing franchise, prints and posters, original watercolors, custom framing. Located mainly in urban and resort locations, targeting corporate and trade accounts as well as tourists.

History: In business since 1968; franchising since 1984; thirty-eight franchised units, fifteen company-owned units.

Cash Investment: $40,000 to $80,000 start-up cash. Franchise fee $15,000 to $25,000.

Training and Support: Training before opening, continues on-site before and after opening. Ongoing support with framing techniques, purchasing, merchandising, and sales. Managerial assistance with site location, lease negotiations, construction, floor plans, store set-up, marketing plan, national vendor accounts, employee policy, and operations manual.

Qualifications: None listed.

Fastframe USA
1200 Lawrence Drive, #300
Newbury Park, CA 91320
Ph: 800-521-3726 or 805-498-4463
Fax: 805-498-8983

Contact: Brian J. Harper, Chief Operating Officer

Type of Business: Custom picture-framing retail stores.

History: In business since 1986; franchising since 1987; 151 franchised units, one company-owned unit.

Cash Investment: $150,000 to $200,000 start-up cash. Franchise fee $25,000. Financial assistance: leasing package ranging from $30,000 to $40,000.

Training and Support: At corporate training center, two weeks of training in retail management and custom framing techniques. Managerial assistance includes marketing, purchasing, operations, and accounting.

Qualifications: Some knowledge of art as well as sales and marketing skills helpful but not required.

Restaurants

KFC Corporation (Kentucky Fried Chicken)
1441 Gardiner Lane
Louisville, KY 40213
Ph: 502-456-8300
Fax: 502-456-8306

Contact: Stephen B. Early, Vice President of Franchise Administration

Type of Business: Quick-service restaurant.

History: In business since 1930; franchising since 1952; 5,964 franchised units, 2,223 company-owned units.

Cash Investment: $150,000 start-up cash, $983,000 to $1,410,000 total investment.

Training and Support: Seven-week training course before opening; continual assistance in customer service, management, quality control, and employee training. Managerial assistance in site selection, engineering and construction, equipment, materials and supplies, etc. Periodic inspections to ensure compliance with standards and specifications.

Qualifications: KFC is currently not recruiting franchises in the United States.

McDonald's Corporation
One McDonald's Plaza, Kroc Drive
Oak Brook, IL 60521
Ph: 708-575-6196
Fax: 708-575-5645

Contact: Franchising Department

Type of Business: Fast-food restaurants.

History: In business since 1955; franchising since 1955; 13,283 franchised units, 3,513 company-owned units.

Cash Investment: Total investment of $408,600 to $647,000 required, of which 40 percent must be from personal, unencumbered funds. Financial requirements vary outside the United States.

Training and Support: Prospective franchisees are required to participate in a training and evaluation program which may, on a part-time basis, take two years or longer to complete. Manuals provided on operations, training, maintenance, accounting, and equipment. Promotional advertising material and field operations support.

Qualifications: Entrepreneurship, ability to train people, completion of training program, and devotion of full-time efforts to business. International candidates are selected from local markets and need local-market business experience.

International: Worldwide—Seventy-nine foreign countries as well as all fifty states and District of Columbia.

Commercial Cleaning/Janitorial Services

Jani-King
Jani-King International, Inc.
4950 Keller Springs Road, Suite 190
Dallas, TX 75248
Ph: 800-552-5264 or 972-991-0900
Fax: 972-991-5723

Contact: Jerry L. Crawford, President

Type of Business: Commercial cleaning system.

History: In business since 1969; franchising since 1974; 6,156 franchised units.

Cash Investment: $2,400 start-up cash; $6,500 to $80,000 total investment required. Franchisor provides the option to finance the total franchise fee.

Training and Support: Training provided for all new franchisees under supervision of technical experts. Ongoing training and support to help franchise owners develop.

Qualifications: No experience required.

International: Africa, Asia, Canada, Europe, and Latin America.

**ServiceMaster, The ServiceMaster Company
860 Ridge Lake Boulevard
Memphis, TN 38120-9792
Ph: 800-255-9687 or 901-684-7500
Fax: 901-684-7600**

Contact: Robert E. Burdge, Director of Franchise Sales

Type of Business: Residential and commercial cleaning services.

History: In business since 1947; franchising since 1952; 4,408 franchised units.

Cash Investment: $8,000 to $15,000 to start up; total investment varies. ServiceMaster will finance up to 70 percent of franchise, supplies, and equipment.

Training and Support: Ten-phase program including manuals and videos, ServiceMaster orientation, self-study, assistance with basic start-up tasks, two weeks of on-the-job training, one week at ServiceMaster Academy of Management, and financial counseling.

Qualifications: None listed.

TRAVEL AGENTS

**CruiseOne, Inc.
10 Fairway Drive, Suite 200
Deerfield Beach, FL 33441
Ph: 800-892-3928 or 954-428-8433
Fax: 954-428-8343**

Contact: Ruben Luna, Vice President, Representative of Licensing

Type of Business: Cruise travel company.

History: In business since 1992; franchising since 1993; 300 franchised units.

Cash Investment: $6,800 to $10,700 start-up cash; $10,700 to $21,050 total investment.

Training and Support: Home study course prior to a five-day intensive training session. Customized software, advanced seminars at national conventions. Marketing department, 800# help lines, newsmagazines, and brochures.

Qualifications: Highly motivated self-starters. Sufficient capital to promote; marketing, sales, and business management capabilities.

Uniglobe Travel
The Uniglobe Building
900-1199 West Pender Street
Vancouver, BC V6E 2R1, Canada
Ph: 800-590-4111
Fax: 614-764-0112

Contact: Director of Franchise Licensing

Type of Business: Full-service retail travel agency.

History: In business since 1980; franchising since 1981; 1,170 franchised units.

Cash Investment: $27,500 start-up cash; $120,000 to $150,000 total investment.

Training and Support: Uniglobe orientation; commercial sales, vacation sales, and group and incentive sales

69

training; international management academy; video-based training; financial management; standardized operation procedures; budget and finance programs.

Qualifications: No travel background necessary. Management or sales background a plus. Entrepreneurial spirit, commitment, dedication, and tenacity are assets.

THE SPECTRUM OF FRANCHISES
These are just a few examples of franchises within several industries. There is an endless array of businesses that are and can be franchised. Franchise categories include:

- accounting/tax services
- advertising/direct mail services
- art supplies
- auto/truck buying and leasing
- auto/truck rentals
- automotive products and services
- beauty salons and supplies
- beverages
- bookstores
- business aids and services
- business brokers
- campgrounds
- check cashing/financial service centers
- chemicals and related products
- children's products and services
- clothing and shoes
- commercial cleaning and janitorial services
- computer/electronics
- construction and remodeling
- convenience stores
- cosmetics and toiletries

- credit reporting services
- dating services
- dental centers
- drugstores
- educational products and services
- employment services
- environmental services
- fire protection
- florist shops
- food (baked goods, candy/snacks, ice cream/yogurt, pizza, specialty)
- formal wear rental
- hair salons and services
- health aids and services
- home furnishings
- home inspection
- hotels and motels
- insurance
- jewelry
- laundry and dry cleaning
- lawn and garden supplies and services
- maid and personal services
- maintenance and sanitation
- optical aids and services
- package preparation and shipping
- painting services
- pest control
- pet sales and supplies
- photography and supplies
- pressure washing and restoration
- printing/photocopying
- publications
- real estate
- recreation equipment and supplies
- recreation services
- recycling products and services

- rental of equipment and supplies
- restaurants
- retail stores
- security systems
- sign products and services
- swimming pools
- tailoring/alterations
- telecommunication services
- tools and hardware
- transportation services
- travel agents
- vending machine services
- video/audio sales and rentals
- vitamin and mineral stores
- water conditioning
- weight control

9

Choosing a Franchise That Is Right for You

Before investing in a particular franchise system, carefully consider how much money you have to invest, your abilities, and your goals. Review the characteristics of an entrepreneur and of a franchisee listed in chapter 4. The following checklist may help in making a decision about franchising.

QUESTIONS AND ANSWERS

Self-Assessment

Questions to ask yourself about the investment:
- How much money do I have available to invest?
- How much money can I afford to lose if my business fails?
- Will I purchase the franchise by myself or will I have partners?
- How much financing will I need, and where will I get it?
- Is my credit rating good?
- Do I have savings or additional income to live on while I start a franchise?

Questions to ask yourself about your abilities:
- Does the franchise require technical experience or a certain kind of education, such as auto

repair, home and office decorating, or tax preparation? Do I have that experience or education? If not, can I get it?
- What skills (computer, bookkeeping, or other technical skills) do I have?
- What specialized knowledge or talents (such as cooking ability, mechanical skills, or a flair for decorating) can I bring to a business?
- Do I have experience in managing or owning a business?

Questions to ask yourself about your goals:
- What are my business goals and general (life) goals?
- How much income will I need each year?
- What kind of work interests me the most? Working with flowers, fixing cars, crunching numbers, helping people, or . . . ?
- Which interests me more, sales or performing a service?
- How many hours am I willing and able to work each day or week?
- Do I want to operate a business myself, or would I rather hire a manager?
- Will the franchise business be my main source of income, or do I expect it to provide me with additional income?
- Will I be happy operating the same business for the next twenty years?

Goodness of Fit

Finding the right franchise may come down to a personality match. Although you must be willing to follow the franchisor's rules, some franchisors are quite open to franchisees' ideas. If you are a people-person who is a good learner, you may be more successful in franchising (with the right training) than someone who has a business background. When you have an interview with the franchisor, he or she should be able to tell you if you are not suited to franchising or to the particular franchise industry you are considering.

Selecting a Franchise
Like any other investment, purchasing a franchise entails risk. When you select a franchise, you must carefully consider a variety of factors. These include the demand for the products or services, the likely competition, the franchisor's background, the level of training and support offered to a franchisee, and the franchise's potential growth.

Questions to ask about demand for the products or services:
- Is there a demand for the franchisor's products or services in the community where I would operate the franchise?
- Is the demand for the product or service seasonal in the location where I would operate the franchise? For example, there is no winter demand for lawn and garden care or swimming maintenance in areas of the country where snow and cold temperatures are typical winter weather.
- Is it probable that there will be a continuing demand for the franchisor's products or services in the future? Is the demand likely to be temporary, such as sales of a current fad item?
- Does the product or service create repeat business?

Questions to ask about competition:
- What is the level of competition in my community, in the region, and nationally?
- How many franchised and company-owned outlets does the franchisor have in my area?

- How many other companies sell the same or similar products or services?
- Are these competing companies well established, with wide name recognition in the community?
- Do the competing companies offer the same goods or services at the same or lower price?

Questions to ask yourself about your ability to operate the business:
- Will I be able to operate my business if the franchisor goes out of business?
- Will I need the franchisor's ongoing training, advertising, or other assistance to succeed, or can I get the help I need from someone else?
- If the franchisor goes out of business, will I be able to get the supplies I need, either from the franchisor's supplier or elsewhere?
- Could I run the business by myself if I had to lay off my employees to save on costs?

What's in It for You?

The main reason for purchasing a franchise is your right to associate with the company's name. The more widely recognized the name, the more likely you will have customers who know the franchise's products or services.

Questions to ask about the franchise's name recognition:
- How widely is the company's name recognized?
- Is the name a registered trademark?
- How long has the franchisor been in operation?
- Does the company have a reputation for quality products or services?
- Have consumers filed complaints against the franchise with the Better Business Bureau or a local consumer protection agency?

Questions to ask about training and support:
- What training and ongoing support will the franchisor provide?
- How does the training compare with the training usually provided for workers in that industry who are not involved in a franchise? (This question is particularly important if you do not have a background in a franchise that requires special skills, for example, automotive maintenance.)
- What costs will be associated with training? (You will probably have travel costs, including food and lodging, if you go to another location for training.)
- With the training offered by the franchisor, could I compete with others who may have more formal training?
- What kinds of backgrounds do the current franchisees have?
- Did many of the franchisees have technical backgrounds or special training that helped them succeed? If so, is my background similar?

Before You Commit

You have no guarantee that a person who successfully started a business can successfully manage a franchise system. If a franchisor has little experience in managing a chain of franchises, any promises of guidance, training, and other support may not be reliable.

Questions to ask about the franchise company:
- How long has the franchisor been in business?
- How long has the franchisor managed a franchise system?
- Do I feel comfortable with the franchisor's expertise?

- How many franchised outlets are there? Where are they located?
- How much is the initial franchise fee and any additional start-up costs?
- Will I have to make royalty payments? If so, how much?
- What controls will the franchisor put on my business?
- If the franchise company grows quickly, is the franchisor likely to have enough financial assets and staff to provide support?
- Does the franchise company require or, at least, recommend that I meet with current franchisees? (The franchisor should encourage you to find out how the system really works by talking with people who are working within it.)
- Does the representative of the franchise company act in a professional manner? (The professionalism, or lack of it, reflects that of the company.)
- Does the franchisor's representative closely examine my qualifications and suitability for the franchise? (The franchisor owes it to current franchisees to accept only qualified applicants.)
- Is there a franchisees' association that will provide me with contact with the franchisor's other franchisees? (Such associations also give franchisees an opportunity to solve problems together and to decide how to act on issues that affect all of them.)

SHOPPING AT A FRANCHISE EXPOSITION

A franchise exposition gives you the opportunity to look at and compare a variety of franchise possibilities. Keep in mind that exhibitors want to sell their franchise systems. Before attending an exposition, research which type of franchises suit your investment limitations, experience, interests, and goals. At the exhibition, comparison shop for the franchise opportunity that fits your needs and abilities. Visit several exhibitors in the type of industry that interests you and ask questions.

Pick up promotional literature and exhibitors' business cards. When you return home and the excitement of the exhibition is behind you, you can spend time reading the materials you picked up. If you have questions, you can call a specific person whose card you brought home. It's also a good idea to take along paper and pen in order to take notes. Some exhibitors may offer prizes, free samples, or free dinners at a promotional meeting. If you choose to accept any of these offers, do not feel obligated to the franchisor. Instead, consider the meetings as an opportunity to get more information and to ask questions.

If you find that a franchise does not suit your needs and abilities, walk away from it. Do not feel pressured to make a commitment during the exposition. Some franchisors may say that their offering is limited, that only one territory is left, or that the franchise sales price has been temporarily reduced. Legitimate franchisors, however, expect you to investigate and compare several franchises.

Some franchisors may talk about how much money their franchisees earn. They use general statements such as "high sales to investment ratio," "a higher profit margin," "among top volume performers" or "adds up to an extremely attractive profit potential." Such talk is expected in business sales and is not considered fraudulent. If a franchisor makes actual earnings claims, the FTC requires that written documentation of the claims be provided in the Uniform Franchise Offering Circular (UFOC). If that is not done, you should remove the franchise from your list of possibilities. Do not sign a contract or make any payment until you have the opportunity to investigate the franchisor's offering completely. (This topic is discussed in more detail in chapters 10 and 11.)

You can use several kinds of resources to answer the questions in this chapter. The resources are discussed in chapter 10.

Bob Vennell, Jani-King

"When I worked late hours at Dun & Bradstreet in New York, I saw janitorial services not doing the job well, and I knew they were well paid," Bob Vennell recalls. "I moved with Dun & Bradstreet many times in ten years, and I saw the same substandard performance, theft, and no-shows everywhere. I thought it couldn't be that hard to do well and make money doing it."

When Bob decided he wanted to leave the corporate world, where he had risen to the position of regional manager, he considered franchises in several industries—car service and maintenance, printing and copying, janitorial services, and fast food. He investigated several opportunities in each industry. He asked to see their UFOCs and compared them in detail. He knew he wanted to operate his business from home, so he also inquired about city and state permits.

"I wanted a business in which I'd be working hands-on," he says, "and one that would provide us with income in one year. My wife and I had saved enough money to live on for one year, and she also had income from real estate sales."

Bob knew what a successful business should look like. He had taken business courses in college and had worked as a business analyst. When he compared the UFOCs of various franchise companies, he found many differences, including cost. He knew he was not in a position to spend $300,000 on a franchise. He chose Jani-King because it was affordable, and he knew there was a demand for commercial janitorial service.

Bob bought and started up his Jani-King franchise in 1987 for $25,000, a low cost that is still possible to find today. Jani-King provided part of the financing. For this, Bob received cleaning equipment, an initial inventory of cleaning compounds, manuals, and training. The training began with reading the manuals, followed by one week of hands-on training in Dallas, Texas.

"In Dallas I learned about equipment like the floor machine, about cleaning systems and chemicals, about business operations such as employee training and management, and how to bid a cleaning contract on a building," Bob recalls. "I opened the franchise in July 1987, operating it out of my home.

"I needed help on bidding for my first contract, so I called the toll-free 800 number," Bob says. "I had measured the building, I knew how much was carpet and how much was floor, I knew the bathroom, the trash, etc., but I still needed to be walked through the actual bid. I also had questions about equipment, which I can buy from a Jani-King supplier or an independent local vendor."

With a home-based business, Bob didn't have to consider the cost of leasing or renting a franchise location.

To bring in business, he contacted people he knew in the corporate world, and his wife's real estate contacts. After about six months he was able to begin taking personal income from the business profits, well before his goal of one year.

Bob has always worked fifty to sixty hours a week, but now his responsibilities have changed. In 1991, he bought the master franchise rights for the state of Washington and he has more than fifty franchisees for whom he provides training and support.

"I still spend about 10 percent of my time cleaning," Bob says. *"Last week I was running a floor polisher just to help a franchisee start off on the right foot with a new customer."*

10

Getting Help Before Getting Started

Buying a franchise with name recognition and a proven system of doing business will not guarantee you a profit. With this in mind, you should approach the purchase of a franchise with your eyes wide open, looking for as much information as you can get. Every franchisor must provide a prospective franchisee with a written document—the Uniform Franchise Offering Circular (UFOC). Before making the decision to purchase a specific franchise, you should examine a variety of opportunities, examine specific franchises and each franchisor, and analyze and evaluate the criteria in the UFOC for each franchise.

KNOW YOUR MARKET

To help you determine whether the product or service has the potential for a long-term market, a franchisor should provide a profile of the ideal market. The profile should include size and average age of the population, household income, and discretionary spending. Many franchisors have territories for their franchisees that meet the profile criteria.

You should also check out the market in other ways. U.S. Census statistics, which are available in public libraries, provide demographic data about the population. Unfortunately, because a census is done only every decade, the statistics can be almost ten years old.

However, you can get more up to date information from market research firms, which update, forecast, and analyze census statistics for specific geographic areas or for the entire nation.

Some products and services are more successful in certain parts of the country than in others. It's important to understand the customs, tastes, traditions, and wealth of a community before opening a business there. You can get a community profile at a library, the Chamber of Commerce for that region, or the city government office. The profile will include statistics about the population by ethnic group, per capita income, job growth, and traffic patterns, as well as planned growth and construction.

You can also get information from industry trade associations. For example, if you are interested in purchasing a dry-cleaning franchise, you could contact the International Fabricare Institute to learn about the industry outlook. You can also conduct your own marketing survey by speaking with franchisors of similar products or services if you are considering opening a printing franchise. For example, you can find the names and locations of printers in your local Yellow Pages. Ask the printers who are already in business about their plans for expansion. You might also speak with customers leaving the business (in the parking lot) and ask about their satisfaction with the company's quality and loyalty to that particular brand name.

SELECTING THE BEST FRANCHISE WITHIN AN INDUSTRY

The next step is to compare franchises within the industry you have selected. Information on the franchise companies that interest you should be listed in Dun & Bradstreet reports, which are available at libraries or through your banker.

The IFA's resources include a database of franchise

opportunities that has links to company Web sites; a resource center that can provide helpful articles on franchising; and *Franchising World* magazine, which reports on trends within the franchise community and offers the latest information on franchising along with e-mail links to all IFA members.

You also may find some assurance in the four-page Code of Principles and Standards of Conduct that IFA members follow. The IFA requires franchisor members to develop fair and effective dispute resolution procedures, to publicize the existence of the procedures within their franchise networks, and to make good-faith efforts to resolve disputes with franchisees. When a member violates the code, the IFA requires the member to adopt procedures and policies that will reduce the likelihood of future violations. The organization receives fewer than fifty complaints a year. Although it may suspend or terminate IFA membership for members whose policies and practices reflect a consistent disregard of the code, the president, Don DeBolt, says no complaint has ever resulted in the removal of a member.

Other sources of information include attorneys, accountants, banks and other financial institutions, the Better Business Bureau, government departments, and the FTC.

Understanding the Contract

Franchise contracts are usually long and complex. A problem that comes up after you sign the contract may be very costly and might be impossible to amend. Before signing any agreement, you should have an attorney with franchise experience examine the contract. The attorney should point out if there are any franchise requirements that may be unwise, illegal, or unethical. Sections of a contract that make you uncomfortable at the beginning of a business relationship are more likely to result in problems later. An attorney can also identify and advise you about legal technicalities connected with the business contract.

How an Accountant Can Help

An accountant can help you pick a franchise system that is best suited to your business goals and investment resources. An accountant can help you understand the franchise company's financial statements, develop a business plan, and assess any earnings projections and the assumptions upon which they are based. Your accountant should answer the following questions:

- Is the initial investment for the franchise fee, equipment, and location reasonable?
- Do ratio tables of typical expenditures for certain categories of business indicate that the royalties and cooperative advertising rates are reasonable?
- Is the investment a reasonable risk? (Using a form called a financial pro forma, the accountant should work with you to develop a five-year business plan. The financial proforma helps balance out three areas: personal assets, resources for financing the franchise, and the potential return on investment.)

It is best for you to have your own attorney and accountant rather than depending on attorneys or accountants provided by the franchisor.

Other Helping Hands

Banks: Banks and other financial institutions can also provide an unbiased view of the franchise opportunity.

Bankers have ready access to Dun & Bradstreet or similar reports on the franchisor and can explain the information in the reports. Information in chapter 12 shows how a banker can also offer a perspective on the business opportunity and on the franchisor in particular.

The Better Business Bureau: The Better Business Bureau in the city where the franchisor has headquarters, will have information on whether any consumers have complained about the company's products, services, or personnel.

SCORE: Members of the Service Corps of Retired Executives offer free general and specific business advice. Such advice is also available free or at low cost from small-business development centers, which are often part of city or county government or a service of a college or university. Check the Yellow Pages for listings of the Small Business Association near you.

You should also check with state and local consumer protection boards and with franchise regulators in the fifteen states that require state registration. They are California, Hawaii, Illinois, Indiana, Maryland, Michigan, Minnesota, New York, North Dakota, Oregon, Rhode Island, South Dakota, Virginia, Washington, and Wisconsin. You should be aware that federal and state rules do not prevent a franchisor from taking certain actions that can affect your profits. Many contracts do not address such factors as the opening of a competing unit nearby, the forcing of franchisees to buy supplies at greatly inflated prices, or imposition of severe terms for contract renewal. Every state's Division of Securities or Office of Attorney General can provide information about a franchisee's rights in the state.

SELF-DEFENSE

Don't Wait to Investigate

The FTC publishes information that may be helpful as you investigate franchising opportunities and move toward the contract stage. A list of more than 100 free ftc publications on business and consumer topics, such as "Getting Business Credit," may be obtained free of charge by writing to Public Reference, Federal Trade Commission, Washington, DC 20580. Although the ftc does not resolve individual disputes, information a franchisee provides about problems with a franchisor helps the agency in its enforcement efforts. The FTC will disclose past law enforcement actions against franchisors but will not comment on pending investigations or current complaints. FTC headquarters and regional offices are listed in the back of this book. Other government agencies provide books, pamphlets, and advice on how to protect yourself from unscrupulous businesspeople.

Protecting Yourself Against Fraud

The National District Attorneys Association (NDAA) has published helpful warning signs of possible business opportunity fraud. The NDAA lists five "red flags" that should put you on guard. Although the tactics listed do not mean that the franchise offer is fraudulent, they are typical fraudulent tactics. You should be wary of any opportunity that is based on them.

- If a franchisor offers you a deal to earn high income in your spare time, you may be purchasing materials or instructions for projects that are worthless.
- If the franchisor offers you a business opportunity that depends primarily on the sale of

subfranchises and royalties from sublicenses, rather than the sale of products or services, the deal is likely to be a pyramid scheme.

- If a franchisor advertises one operation or product but then suggests a switch to another that is better, more expensive or cheaper, safer, or in some way different, the deal is likely to be a bait-and-switch routine.
- Be sure to learn the franchise company's actual name. If a franchisor has a name almost like that of a well-known company—Hardies (Hardee's), Mail Box Service (Mail Boxes Etc.) or One Globe Travel (Uniglobe Travel)—the franchisor's intention may be to mislead you into thinking you are dealing with a well-known company.
- If the franchisor discourages you from seeking independent professional advice and assistance (such as from an attorney or an accountant), you definitely need to get it.

Before You Sign on the Dotted Line...

You should get all promises in writing, ask for permission to tape-record conversations with the franchisor, and have all of your questions answered to your satisfaction before signing anything or parting with any money. Do not allow yourself to be rushed into making a decision. In fact, if a person who represents a franchise company attempts to rush you, you should be suspicious of the company itself. You should also give extra scrutiny to a company that holds meetings in hotel rooms or temporary offices. Keep in mind, however, that impressive offices and a wall of framed licenses and certificates do not guarantee a company's integrity.

A franchisor's disclosure papers—the UFOC—are an important source of information. The franchisor must provide this document at one of three times, whichever comes first: at the first face-to-face meeting with you or at the time you set for making disclosures regarding the terms and conditions of the sale of the franchise; ten days prior to your making any payment to the franchisor; or ten days prior to the signing of any contract that commits you to buy the franchise.

Make certain that you see these papers before you sign anything, and be sure to have an attorney review the disclosure papers and any and all agreements that you are to sign. It may cost you a few hundred dollars to hire an attorney, but it will definitely be worth it by protecting you from entering into a risky arrangement.

11

Pursuing a Franchise Possibility

THE UFOC
When you investigate and compare franchise opportunities, you have a valuable tool in the disclosure papers. You can compare "apples with apples" rather than "apples with oranges" because the UFOCs of franchisors in the same industry have the same basic format. Every UFOC must be valid for the current fiscal year and identify the business that is being franchised and the amounts of the initial franchise fees.

How to Read a UFOC
The front page identifies whether the UFOC is published according to federal law or state law, or both. The first page should state that it is being provided for the reader's protection and that it contains a summary of certain material provisions of the franchise agreement. The UFOC should include the following information as well.

The business background and record of the franchisor and key management staff.
This section includes the background of the current franchisor and his or her predecessors. With this information, you should be able to run a credit check on the company and its officers. Information about their previous businesses, including other franchise businesses, will help you determine if they have a proven track

record. They should have enough experience to be able to add to your own business expertise, whatever it may be. They also should have special knowledge of the type of business they are in. When you know about their experience and specialized knowledge, you will have a better idea about the likelihood of your own success with the franchise business operation they are selling. Your risk is likely to be higher if you invest with an inexperienced franchisor.

The franchisor's involvement in any past or current litigation or bankruptcy proceedings.
The UFOC states whether the franchisor or any of the executive officers have been convicted of felonies, such as fraud, violation of franchise law, or unfair or deceptive practices. It also states whether the franchisor or executive officers are subject to any state or federal injunctions for similar misconduct. You should be extremely cautious about entering into a contract with any franchisor or franchise company whose key employees have been convicted of crimes or have had major court judgments made against them.

The UFOC also states whether the franchisor or executives have been held liable in or settled a civil action involving the franchise. You should be aware that some franchisors may try to conceal an executive's litigation history by removing that person's name from the UFOC. A number of claims against the franchisor may indicate that the company has not performed according to its agreements or that franchisees have been dissatisfied with the franchisor's performance. If the UFOC shows that the franchisor has been involved in litigation, you should contact the current or past franchisees involved in the litigation or their attorneys to hear their side of the story. Also ask the franchisor to explain the litigation.

The UFOC states whether the franchisor or any executives have recently been involved in bankruptcy. This information helps you assess the franchisor's financial stability and general business ability. It may also suggest that the company may not be financially capable of delivering the support services it promises to franchisees.

The franchise company's financial history.

The UFOC provides information about the company's financial status, including audited financial statements. It is important to realize that investing in a financially unstable franchisor is a major risk. The company may go out of business or into bankruptcy after you have invested money. It is essential to hire a lawyer or accountant to review the franchisor's financial statements, because it is difficult for a person without considerable financial background to extract this information from the UFOC. The lawyer or accountant should be able to explain the following information and what it indicates for the success of the franchisee.

- Does the franchisor have steady growth?
- Does the franchisor have a growth plan?
- Does the franchising company make most of its income from the sale of franchises or from continuing royalties?
- Does the franchisor provide sufficient funds to the support of its franchise system?

Initial and recurring costs paid by the franchisee.

The UFOC describes the costs involved in starting one of the company's franchises. It describes any initial deposit or franchise fee, which may be nonrefundable, and costs for initial inventory, signs, equipment, leases, or rentals. There may be other costs that are not disclosed in the UFOC. Use the following checklist for asking questions about potential costs.

- Continuing royalty payments (typically 5 to 15 percent of gross, not net, revenues).
- Advertising payments to local and to national advertising funds (usually 3 to 8 percent of gross revenues).
- Grand opening or other initial business promotions.
- Business or operating licenses.
- Product or service supply costs.
- Required sublease of franchised premises from the franchisor.
- Real estate and leasehold improvements.
- Discretionary equipment such as a computer system or alarm system.
- Training costs.
- Legal fees that the franchisor requires franchisees to pay.
- Any costs for financial and accounting advice
- Insurance.
- Compliance with local ordinances, such as zoning, waste removal, environmental codes, and fire and other safety codes.
- Employees salaries and benefits, such as health insurance.

When you contact current franchisees to learn about the business, ask if they were satisfied with the benefits they received for their initial fee. You may need to contact city, county, state, or federal agencies for answers about costs for advice and insurance.

The number of franchises, including company-owned outlets. The UFOC includes information about current franchisees, which helps you determine the number of franchises currently operating. A large number of franchisees in the area where you plan to locate may indicate that there will be too much competition.

Details of the franchise agreement dealing with renewal and termination terms, as well as the number of franchises terminated within the past year and the reasons for termination.

The disclosure statement states the conditions under which the franchisor may terminate your franchise and your obligations to the franchisor after termination. It also states the conditions under which you can renew, sell, or assign the franchise to other parties. The more limitations that exist for you, the more difficult it will be for you to recover your money if you decide you do not want to continue in the franchise. Many franchisors will offer to buy back the franchise under certain conditions. It is important to understand clearly what the buyback provision involves.

You should also consider what must happen for you or the franchisor to cancel the contract. It should be a reasonable and clear process. You should also ask whether the franchiser will agree to buy back the franchise if it is canceled. Without this provision, you may lose all of your initial investment. You also should ask if, when a contract is canceled, the franchisor will pay for the goodwill you developed with customers during the course of the business.

Franchisors sometimes buy out or close unsuccessful franchisees to remove problems from the system. If this has happened to a significant number of franchisees, it suggests a problem within the franchisor's system and a greater risk for a new franchisee. The UFOC lists the names and addresses of franchisees who have left the franchise system within the past year. It is a good idea to speak with these people to learn why they left.

When time for the "renewal" of the franchise agreement arrives, most franchisees find that the existing agreement is not renewed. Instead, they enter into a new franchise agreement, often with substantially different financial and operating terms.

A description of available training programs and other assistance. Be sure to understand the level of training offered. The best programs include a combination of classroom training and on the job (on-site) training. A program of several weeks is most effective. The following checklist will help you ask the right questions.

- Who pays for the training? Who pays for materials, lodging, meals, and travel to the training sessions?
- How much of the franchisee's employees are eligible for training?
- Can employees hired after start-up receive training, and if so, is there a cost to the franchisee?
- How long are the training sessions?
- How much time is spent on technical training, management training, marketing training?
- Who teaches the training courses, and what are their qualifications?
- What type of ongoing training does the company offer? What is the cost to franchisees?
- If a franchisee has a problem, whom can he or she consult?
- How many support staff has the franchisor assigned to the area in which you plan to open your business? How many franchisees does each support person work with?
- If necessary, would support staff be able to come to the franchised outlet to provide more individual assistance?

- Will the franchisor help the franchisee in obtaining financing? If the franchisor provides the financing, does it include the franchise fee, equipment, building, supplies, and operating capital? What are the interest rate and loan conditions? (The franchisee's attorney or accountant should check the loan conditions.)
- How will the franchisor help the franchisee choose a location? What assistance is provided in constructing a building economically, and is there a charge for the assistance?

As discussed in chapter 5, the level of training you need depends on your business experience as well as knowledge of the franchisor's goods and services. Keep in mind that a major reason for investing in a franchise is training and assistance. If you have doubts that the training is adequate for handling day-to-day business operations, you should consider another franchise more suited to your background.

Restrictions

The franchisor may restrict how you operate the outlet. The UFOC indicates whether the franchisor limits the following aspects of the business:

- The supplier of goods from whom you may purchase. You should beware of a franchise in which the suppliers are relatives or friends of the franchisor. This could result in inflated, noncompetitive prices.
- The goods or services you may offer for sale.
- The territory in which you may sell the goods or services and the customers to whom you can offer them.
- Rules about personal participation in the franchise and absentee management.

Advertising

A franchisee must often contribute a percentage of income to an advertising fund, despite disagreement with how the funds are used. The UFOC provides information on advertising costs. The following checklist is helpful in assessing whether the franchisor's advertising is likely to benefit you.

- How much of the advertising fund is spent on administrative costs?
- Are other expenses paid from the advertising fund?
- Do franchisees have any control over how advertising dollars are spent?
- What kinds of advertising promotions has the company engaged in?
- What advertising developments are expected in the near future?
- How much of the fund is spent on national advertising? Regional?
- How much of the fund is spent on advertising in the area where you plan to open your business?
- Is the advertising professionally prepared?
- Is there a marketing strategy that maximizes the use of various media, such as newspapers, radio, television, billboards?
- How much of the fund is spent on promoting the sale of more franchises?
- Do all franchisees contribute equally to the advertising fund?
- Is the franchisor's consent needed for a franchisee to do his or her own advertising apart from that provided by the franchisor?
- Are there rebates or advertising contribution discounts if the franchisee does his or her own advertising?
- Does the franchisor receive any commissions or

rebates when placing advertisements? If so, do franchisees benefit, or does only the franchisor profit from them?

Current and Former Franchisees.
This list should appear in every UFOC. Some franchisors, however, may provide a separate reference list of selected franchisees to contact. Those on the list may be paid by the franchisor to give a good opinion of the company. The following checklist will help you ask important questions when you contact current and former franchisees.

- How long has the franchisee operated the franchise?
- Where is the franchise outlet located?
- What was the franchisee's total investment for start-up?
- Were there any hidden or unexpected costs—equipment, signs, logos—or were the actual costs the same as those stated in the UFOC?
- Is the franchise profitable? How long did it take to cover operating costs and earn a reasonable income? Has the franchisee made the profit he or she expected to make? (Compare these figures with any earnings statement the company provided.)
- Is the franchisee satisfied with the cost, delivery, and quality of the goods or service he or she is selling? (Ask to see a price list. Does it reflect the actual costs?)
- What was the franchisee's background, experience, and education?
- Was the franchisor's training adequate? What is the franchisee's assessment of the training?
- What exactly were the training programs, on-site

99

assistance, site selection, and feasibility studies provided?

- Have the operations manuals provided by the franchisor been helpful? Are they changed frequently? If so, why?
- What ongoing assistance does the franchisor provide? What assistance does the franchisee consider the most valuable, and why?
- Is the franchisee satisfied with the advertising program? How effective has the franchisor's advertising been in promoting business? Is it worth the advertising royalties?
- What are the franchisor's territorial restrictions and protections? Does the franchisee believe the results are positive or negative?
- How long are the franchisee's workdays and workweeks? Does the franchisee take vacations?
- Does the franchisor fulfill all contractual obligations?
- Is the franchisor fair and easy to work with? Ask for examples.
- Does the franchisor listen to the franchisee's concerns, ideas, and suggestions? Does the franchisor respond to problems and questions in a timely manner?
- Has the franchisee had any disputes with the franchisor? If so, were they settled to the franchisee's satisfaction? How were they settled?
- If the franchisee could go back in time, would he or she make the same decision about buying the franchise? If not, why not?
- If the franchisee has had the chance to renew the franchise agreement, were there any problems?
- Is there a franchisees' association within the company?
- Would the franchisee invest in another outlet?

- Would the franchisee recommend the investment to someone with your goals, income
  requirements, and background?
- Does the franchisee know of any trouble the
  franchisor has had with other franchisees, com-
  petitors, local authorities, or the state or federal
  government?

EARNINGS POTENTIAL

Franchisors are not required to make earnings claims,
but if they do, the FTC's Franchise Rule requires them
to have a reasonable basis for the claims. The franchisor
may not make any statements about profits and sales in
the UFOC or otherwise, unless the statements are
backed up by a detailed written statement. Earnings
claims must be accompanied by a statement that sup-
porting evidence is available on request. The percentage of franchised units that achieve the claimed results
and their locations should be included.

You should review an earnings claim document with
an accountant and possibly with another business advisor, such as a member of SCORE or a small-business
development center. Consider the following points in
reviewing any earnings claims.

Sample Size

A franchisor may claim that franchisees earned a certain amount ($45,000, for example) the previous year.
This claim may be deceptive if only a few franchisees
earned that income and it does not represent typical
earnings. It is important to ask how many franchisees
were included in the number.

Average Incomes

The franchisor may claim that the franchisees earn an
average income of $60,000 a year. Average figures do

not provide information about how individual franchisees perform. A few very successful franchisees can
inflate the average, making the franchise system look
more successful than it is.

Gross Sales
Some franchisors provide figures for the gross sales
revenues of their franchisees. These figures do not
provide information about the franchisees' costs and
resulting profits. A franchise business with high gross
sales revenue on paper may be losing money because
of high expenses.

Net Profits
This is the vital financial aspect. It is important to dis-
cuss net profits with current and former franchisees.
Franchisors often do not have information on net profits of their franchisees. If you do not receive net profit
statements, you should ask the franchisor for this information on company-owned outlets. Remember, however, that company-owned outlets may have lower costs
and higher profits because they can buy equipment,
inventory, and other items in larger quantities. They
may also own rather than lease the property.

Geographic Relevance
Franchise earnings may vary in different parts of the
country. An A & W Restaurant in North Dakota does
not have the volume of year-round business of an A &
W Restaurant in southern California. It's important to
get information on franchise income in the area where
you plan to locate your business.

Franchisees' Backgrounds
Franchisees have varying levels of education, experience, and skills. Franchisees with advanced technical or

business backgrounds can succeed where other, more typical franchisees may not. The success of some franchisees is no guarantee of your success. When you talk with current franchisees, try to find several with backgrounds similar to yours.

THE DOZEN WORST FRANCHISE AGREEMENT PROVISIONS

You can avoid pitfalls by making sure the franchise agreement won't put you at a disadvantage. The American Franchisee Association (AFA) has compiled a list of the twelve worst franchise agreement provisions. The list was prepared by an attorney who specializes in franchise law:

- Preventing a franchisee from talking with anyone outside the franchise system about the franchise experience.
- Requiring legal disputes to be litigated and arbitrated in the home state of the franchisor.
- Allowing a franchisor too much time to correct a default.
- Noncompetition agreements that give the franchisor an unfair advantage.
- Requiring the franchisee to buy all products from the franchisor or the franchisor's suppliers.
- Requiring the franchisee to sublease the franchised premises from the franchisor.
- The franchisor's lack of accountability for advertising funds.
- Requiring the franchisee to pay the franchisor's legal expenses if there is litigation between the two.
- Kickbacks to the franchisor from vendors whose goods or services the franchisee must buy.
- Mandatory arbitration in the case of a dispute.
- Radically different franchise agreements on renewal.

- Changes in the franchise operations manual or other company policies without notice to or consent from the franchisee.

Although some very successful franchises include at least one of these provisions in the franchise agreement, you should try to get the provisions changed before signing a franchise agreement.

12

Financing a Franchise

Several financing options are available for franchise start-ups and for franchisees who want to expand. These include direct financing or a loan guarantee from the franchisor, a loan from the Small Business Administration (SBA), a commercial bank loan, and other sources, such as venture capital firms. All lenders look for a strong business plan and expect you, the borrower, to provide about one-third of the total capital needed to begin the business. This means that for a franchise that costs $12,000 to start up, you must contribute $4,000 from personal sources, such as savings, personal property, stocks, bonds, pension plans, or IRAs. For a franchise costing $45,000, you must contribute $15,000; for a $600,000 franchise, your personal contribution should be $200,000.

WHERE TO BEGIN
You should follow five steps to qualify for financial assistance: determine your net worth, determine your credit potential, develop a business plan, consider the major sources of financing available to you, and select and pursue the most likely source.

Your Net Worth
Net worth is determined by subtracting liabilities from assets. Most banks and lending institutions have a printed form that can be used in preparing this analysis.

The Four Cs

Some lenders use the four Cs of credit in determining your credit potential.

Credit Rating: A banker can suggest whom to contact for a copy of your credit report. It is a record of your credit history over the past few years. Poor credit history is the number one reason for loans not being approved.

Capacity: The banker or other loan officer will want to know if your business will have the earning capacity to pay back the loan. The loan officer will also want to know what assets you will use to make the payments if the business does not provide the necessary cash flow.

Capability: The loan officer will want to know if you are capable of managing the business you want to start and what skills you have that will help make it successful.

Character: The fourth C is character. The loan officer will want to know if you have shown character and integrity in your past business dealings. Character includes your credit history, which shows whether you pay your bills on time. If you had a problem in the past but are currently paying your bills on time, your loan may still be approved. Character also involves your general integrity in the community. When a loan application is on the line between being approved and being rejected, the loan officer usually makes the decision based on character.

The Fifth C

If the bank approves your application for a loan, it will expect security, called *collateral*. This could include equipment, the building in which the business will be located, accounts receivable, inventory, or personal real estate and stocks. The lender will want to know the value of your collateral in case you are not able to repay the loan and the bank has to foreclose and sell the collateral at auction value. That is usually considerably less than what you paid for the equipment and inventory. In most cases, you will need to use personal assets, such as your home, stocks, or bonds, as part of the collateral.

The Business Plan

The third step in applying for financial assistance is the development of a business plan. A banker or loan officer will want to see the following information:

1. A description of the business
   a) Brief description of the franchise
   b) Nature of the business
2. An analysis of the businesses that will be your competition
3. Reasons that the business will succeed
   a) Location
   b) Population factors
   c) Comparison with other similar businesses
4. Methods for generating business
   a) How you will sell your product or service
   b) Advertising and marketing methods
5. A résumé of past business experience, including positions held and any management experience you have had.
6. An estimate of start-up costs. This includes the costs of the franchise fee, building, fixtures and equipment, installation of fixtures and equipment, telephone installation, utility deposits, insurance, licenses and permits, supplies, initial inventory, advertising and promotion, signs, vehicles, and advice from professionals such as an attorney and an accountant.

7. An estimate or projection of income and expenses for one year. Your income projection should be based on information obtained from interviewing current franchisees and from specific information provided by the franchisor (if the franchisor makes income claims). A monthly expense list will help you estimate your expenses for one year. The list should include the amount you will need to take out of the business for personal living expenses and any of the following items that apply: employee wages and fringe benefits, payroll taxes, building mortgage payment or rent, maintenance, utilities, insurance, advertising, supplies, postage and shipping, transportation, inventory replacement, taxes, and royalty payments.

How to Obtain Funding

The next step in obtaining financing is to make a list of all possible sources for the one-third of the financing that you must provide. The list might include a second mortgage on your home, loans from friends or relatives, money from savings accounts, advances on credit cards, and loans borrowed against insurance, stocks, and securities. A list of sources for a major loan would include the SBA, banks, savings and loan institutions, venture capitalists, and possibly even the franchisor.

The final step in obtaining financing is to approach the best financing source with your business plan and personal statement of net worth.

Franchisor Financing

About one-third of franchise companies offer some form of financial assistance. Some provide direct financing programs, loan guarantees, and a variety of leasing programs for property and equipment needed to operate the business.

Most franchisors will help you find a bank or other lender. You can expect the franchisor to have some expertise in obtaining financial assistance. At the least, the franchisor should have a list of banks and other lenders with which the company has a good relationship. If the franchisor does not or cannot help you obtain financing, you should probably consider another franchise opportunity.

The Small Business Administration (SBA)

The SBA, a federal government agency, is one of the best sources of financing available to franchisees. It offers competitive interest rates and generally longer repayment terms than other funding sources. SBA loans are typically made by a bank or other lending institution, with a portion of the loan guaranteed by the SBA.

Call the district SBA office listed in your telephone directory and ask for information about the top SBA lenders in your district. To determine their interest in making you an SBA-guaranteed loan, contact the lenders about your plans. Keep track of which banks have showed the most interest in working with you, and prepare to present your request to the most interested bank.

The SBA offers many loan guarantee programs that meet a variety of small-business needs. The programs include the 7(a) Guaranteed Business Loan Program, the Low Documentation (LowDoc) Loan Program, the Certified Development Company (CDC), and the Small Business Investment Companies (SBICs).

In the 7(a) Guaranteed Business Loan Program, the SBA guarantees loans made by banks and other lending institutions. The SBA has also authorized Small Business Lending Companies to operate under the program. Many SBLCs are among the top lenders of SBA loans, and some have divisions that specialize in franchises.

The LowDoc program requires only a one-page application, and the loan is approved or denied usually within three days of application. The program is an off-shoot of the 7(a) Guaranteed Business Loan Program. Any small business eligible under 7(a) can apply for a LowDoc loan.

The CDC is a private, nonprofit organization licensed by the SBA as a source of loans for small and medium-sized businesses. The loans are available for industrial or commercial buildings or for the purchase of machinery or equipment. The advantage of the program is that you obtain two loans and need to make only a 10 percent down payment. A primary lender provides up to 50 percent of the mortgaged amount, with the CDC making a fully guaranteed second loan for up to 40 percent of the mortgage.

SBICs are SBA-licensed companies that provide equity capital and financing for long-term debt. They specialize in particular industries and often have greater involvement in the business operation.

Before making a franchise loan, the SBA and the private lender will want to review the UFOC provided by the franchisor, as well as the franchise agreement. These documents contain information that is useful in evaluating a loan request, especially repayment ability.

Commercial Bank Loans

Many commercial banks and other lending institutions make small-business loans without a government guarantee. To apply for a bank loan, you must first know what kind of financing you need. Although loans can be structured in a number of ways, bank loans are of two basic types—short-term and long-term.

Short-Term Loans: These loans are usually used in the start-up phase of a business, when working capital is needed to get the business going. They are not usually used for the purchase of the franchise, equipment, or inventory. Short-term loans are usually set up as notes repayable in one, two, or three months. They may also be set up as a line of credit on which you can draw for a year, after which time it must be paid off and a new line of credit established.

Long-Term Loans: These loans are used for specific purposes, such as purchase of equipment, facilities, or a franchise license. They are made for a specific amount of money and a specific length of time, often several years. Payments are monthly. For a period of time, the borrower may be allowed to pay only the interest, not the principal of the loan.

After deciding what kind of loan or loans you need, make an appointment with a commercial loan officer. Explain your business finance needs and the research you have done on the franchise company. Have your business plan and the UFOC with you. Ask the loan officer to give you a list of other information you need to submit with your application. The list will include your personal financial statement; your personal income tax returns for the three preceding years; a business plan that shows your research into the company; your personal business experience; and how your franchise will fit into the marketplace. The list will also include your projections (the pro forma statement) of how your company will generate funds to repay the loan, how much capital you will contribute, and what other sources of income you have. In addition, you will have to write a letter of request explaining what kind of loan you want, for what amount, how you will allocate and use the loan, and how you will repay it. You may want to include a short history of the franchise company, including how it started, how it has grown, and what products or services it provides. Many franchisors offer business plans that can be modified to suit the local marketplace.

When you have all of the information organized (and not before), arrange another appointment with the loan officer. When you leave the information with the lender, ask how long it will take to receive a response to your application and, if the loan is approved, how long it will take for the funds to be available. If the first bank you approach does not grant the loan, do not give up; try another bank. It is important, however, to make no financial commitment to other businesses or individuals for expenditures until the loan has been approved.

Financing Alternatives

If you do not want to or cannot work with a bank or other traditional lender, you can find other financing alternatives. Venture capital firms usually specialize in certain industries and look for a high return on investment, a short payback period, a substantial share of the business, and fixed buy-back terms at a guaranteed price. Fixed buyback terms are written into the franchise agreement. They describe the method of establishing the price of the franchise if you want to sell it back to the franchisor. Fixed buyback terms stipulate what the franchise will be worth to the franchisor. This may be more or less than the franchise unit would bring on the open market.

Nikki Sells, Express Personnel Services

"When my husband and I decided to purchase a franchise, we cashed in our stock and other investments, and we down-sized our house. We knew we

could get through the first six months of owning a franchise, but if my brother hadn't been a cattle rancher we would not have eaten meat for the first year," Nikki Sells says. The Sellses purchased an Express Personnel Services franchise in 1990 for a cost of $50,000, which is about half of what the franchise costs to start up today. The company provides temporary employee service, recruiting and placement of full-time employees, and executive searches.

Nikki was introduced to Express Personnel Services as an employee. She worked in a new franchise operation, gaining experience in sales as well as temporary and permanent placement. She became a manager and opened the franchise's second unit. Nikki's husband also became involved, and after seven years they were managing several franchise operations.

"We decided to do it ourselves," Nikki says. "We checked into other personnel franchise companies and decided to stay with Express. We knew it was a proven system that worked if it was followed. The proven entity of a franchise corporation helped us get an SBA loan, but I believe we also got it on personal character, because we had no collateral.

"We pay a royalty of 40 percent of our gross profits, which may sound high, but we get many services for that," Nikki explains. "We receive legal support, training on issues such as risk management and workers' compensation, brochures and application forms, and accounting support. The company processes the payroll for temporary placement employees. It saves me having to hire five more employees."

Since buying the franchise in Springfield, Missouri, Nikki has become a regional developer—also called a master franchisee—for parts of three states. She provides sales management on site and by phone, and training on site or at her location. She works a minimum of 60 hours a week.

"Anyone who owns a successful business is a workaholic and enjoys the work," Nikki says. "Franchising has been really good for me. The personnel placement industry has many women franchisees and husband-wife teams. Our best friends are other couples and individuals in Express franchises."

Despite their franchising success, the Sellses haven't forgotten their lean beginnings.

"Every year, on April 30, the anniversary of our grand opening in 1990, we eat peanut butter and jelly on bread, and we have our eleven employees do it too," Nikki says.

13

Buying an Existing Franchise Operation

Chapters 9 through 12 discussed various kinds of franchises, how to choose a franchise that is right for you, the resources you can use in investigating and evaluating franchises, the questions you should ask, and how to get financing for buying a franchise. You know that if you purchase a franchise operation directly from the franchisor, you should receive training and guidance in starting the operation, as well as advice and ongoing support in operating your business.

WHAT TO EXPECT

At this point, you may be wondering what happens during the first six months or year as the owner of a franchise operation. There is no "typical" start-up experience. The experience for a new franchisee varies depending on the industry. If you buy a fast-food franchise, you will have a different experience from a franchisee who provides accounting and tax services. A franchisee with a commercial cleaning business will have little in common with the owner of a florist shop.

You can learn about starting a franchise business in the areas that interest you by talking with current franchisees about their experiences.

Buyer Beware

This chapter explores buying an existing franchise operation from a current franchisee. As you investigate various franchise opportunities, you may find yourself talking with a franchisee who wants to sell the business, or a franchisor you have contacted may refer you to a franchisee whose operation is for sale. Try to learn the reason behind the sale, which may or may not be directly related to the business. The franchisee may want to retire or move to another area, may have lost a partner to death, or may be ill. In these situations, the operation may be financially healthy. If, however, a franchisee wants to sell the business because he or she has been unable to make enough of a profit, you may be buying problems if you buy the business.

You should ask the franchisor how many franchisees have operated the business and over what period of time. A number of owners over a short period of time may indicate that the location is not profitable or that the franchisor has not supported that business with adequate services.

Just the Facts

It is very important to get complete information on the franchise operation you want to buy. You should insist on seeing financial records—and having your accountant review them. You should also investigate the franchisor's relationship with franchisees. If you have not spoken with several of the franchisees, use the questions in chapter 11 to learn about the franchisor's performance. Keep in mind that the franchisee who wants to sell the business may not be willing to jeopardize the sale by saying anything negative about the franchisor.

Vive la Différence!

There is a major difference between purchasing a franchise from a franchisor and buying an existing business from a current franchisee. If you purchase an existing franchise operation, you do not have the safeguards that are required by law in the purchase of a franchise from a franchise company. The current franchisee is not bound by FTC disclosure laws, does not have to provide a UFOC, and is not required to give you actual or projected revenue figures of the business. But you do have some protection. Under most franchise agreements, a franchisee can transfer the franchise only with the franchisor's consent. This protects the franchisor from being in business with a new franchisee who may not have the background or ability to operate the business successfully. You should try to get the UFOC from the franchisor before agreeing to the purchase. Before making any commitments, have an attorney familiar with franchises and an accountant examine the UFOC and the purchase agreement. You should also find out if you will have to pay for training that is required or offered by the franchisor, or if you can get the training at no cost from the franchisee who is selling the business.

How will you know if the current franchisee is asking a fair price for the business? Although there is no set formula for determining a fair price for an existing franchise operation, the rule of thumb is that a business is sold for one year's net (not gross) earnings, plus the value of equipment, fixtures, and inventory. In reality, businesses sell for whatever price a buyer is willing to pay and a seller is willing to accept. You can get advice on the value of the business from a banker who knows the value of similar businesses, from a SCORE member, or from a real estate agent who has experience in the sale of similar businesses.

Secrets of Success

If the franchise operation's records show that it is successful, you will want to know the reason or reasons for its success. If you are the only prospective buyer, you may be allowed to observe the business or even to work in the franchise operation for several weeks before you decide whether you want to purchase it. If other people are interested in the operation, it is unlikely that the seller will allow a "try-it" arrangement.

If the business provides a service, the franchise owner's sales ability or technical skills may be the reasons for the success. You should try to determine if this is the case so that you can analyze whether you have similar abilities. The employees may also be a reason behind the success. Although the seller cannot "sell" the employees, the purchase agreement should include a clause stating that the seller will try to persuade employees to continue working for the new owner. The purchase agreement should also include a "noncompete clause," which guarantees that the seller will not compete with the buyer by operating a similar business in the area. Your attorney will advise you about specific clauses that should be included in the purchase agreement.

You should also make sure that a long-term assumable lease is in existence for the property and that the owner of the property will agree to the transfer of the lease from the seller to you. Ask your attorney to make sure you have a written guarantee that the lease will not expire without possibility of renewal or that the rent will not be drastically increased.

If you buy an existing franchise operation, you will begin a long-term relationship with the franchisor, whether you take over the current agreement or have a new agreement with the franchisor. Before buying an existing franchise business, review the information in chapters 9, 10, and 11 and listen carefully to your attorney's and accountant's advice.

SECTION III

LOOKING AHEAD

14

Franchising Around the World

GOING GLOBAL

Franchising is gaining popularity in all areas of the world, with technology making it easier for companies of all sizes to operate worldwide. In the 1970s, international franchising was in its infancy. In 1971, 156 franchising companies were operating 3,565 franchise units in foreign countries. Today there are more than 400 U.S. companies with more than 40,000 franchise units in foreign markets. The international expansion of U.S. franchise companies has benefited the U.S. economy by leading to a trade surplus of $403 million in franchising fees and royalties.

Some companies, like Uniglobe Travel, were begun with the idea of expanding into an international market. The company was founded in Vancouver, British Columbia, Canada, in 1980. Ten years later, 1,000 Uniglobe franchise operations existed in Canada and the United States, and the first overseas franchise was opened. Gary Charlwood, Uniglobe's founder, chairman, and chief executive officer, predicts that within the first few years of the twenty-first century Uniglobe's overseas franchise outlets will outnumber those in the United States and Canada.

A GROWTH MARKET

There are several reasons for the growth of international franchising. People in many parts of the world have more money to spend and are demanding more products and services. In many countries, as in the United States, the economy is shifting from manufacturing to services. Development of U.S. franchises in Canada and Canadian franchises in the United States is not difficult because franchise structures and contract agreements are similar in both countries.

Several Central and Eastern European countries have made a transition from a socialist-communist economy to one in which competitive business growth is encouraged. Today franchise businesses exist in formerly Communist countries. In fact, franchising opportunities can be found in six of the world's seven continents.

THE IFA: YOUR TICKET ABROAD

The IFA encourages the development of franchise associations in other countries. The *Franchise Opportunities Guide* lists national franchise associations in Argentina, Australia, Austria, Belgium, Brazil, Bulgaria, Canada, Chile, China (Hong Kong), Colombia, Czech Republic, Denmark, Ecuador, Finland, France, Germany, Great Britain, Greece, Guatemala, Hungary, Indonesia, Ireland, Israel, Italy, Japan, Malaysia, Mexico, Netherlands, New Zealand, Norway, Philippines, Poland, Portugal, Romania, Russia, Spain, Singapore, South Africa, Sweden, Switzerland, Turkey, (the former) Yugoslavia, and Zimbabwe.

A franchise company that has been successful in the United States may not have success in another country. Every country has different laws, language, customs, and culture. Franchise company representatives must adjust to each country's unique business and cultural climate.

A U.S. franchising company can begin franchising in other countries in several ways. The franchisor may open company-owned units, develop a joint venture with a businessperson in another country, or contract with franchisees (as in the United States). The most common method is to license master franchisors, a system that has also been proven in the United States. A master franchisor is an agent or extension of the franchise company in a specific geographic area. The master franchisor provides all of the franchisor's services (such as training and support) to franchisees in that area.

Before expanding to another country, the franchise company must be sure the products or services are needed in that country. It would not be profitable to open a car wash in a country where the people who own cars usually have an employee who keeps the car clean. Next, the franchisor must find business contacts, learn the country's culture, be well known in the business community, be socially acceptable, and have a good financial reputation. Other hurdles include local regulations and restrictions, approval by national or regional government officials, obtaining a location, and determining how to price and market the product or service. It is also highly important to register the franchise trademark by name and kind of product in each country. In Europe, however, a franchise company can register with EuroMarque for trademark protection.

Government regulations vary widely. In some countries, an American franchisor may be dismayed by the lack of interest in protecting the environment. In Germany, on the other hand, environmental regulations are designed to protect and clean up the country's rivers. Car washes must be equipped with tanks for holding "used water" and with equipment that purifies the water before discharging it into the environment.

How to Know Where to Go

Franchise opportunities vary in different parts of the world. Let's take a look at five geographic regions—

Asia, the Middle East, Central and Eastern Europe, South America, and Europe in general.

Asia
Asia is fertile ground for franchise development. Franchising is a new idea in most of the continent, where more than half of the earth's people live. Many Asian countries have a rapidly growing middle class that wants products and services and can afford to buy them. Although franchising has been established in Japan and Australia for some time, there are "ground floor" opportunities in China, Indonesia, Korea, Malaysia, and Singapore. The major difficulty in developing a franchise business in an Asian country is strict regulation on foreign investments. The situation began to improve in the 1990s, however, when Malaysia, Singapore, and Indonesia all made laws, founded organizations, and introduced programs to encourage investment by foreigners.

The Middle East
Franchising has enormous potential in the Middle East because some of the people are very wealthy. Political unrest and some anti-American sentiment have not reduced Middle Easterners' demand for American products. A franchisor who plans to develop franchises in the Middle East should be prepared to deal with many delays and bureaucratic procedures, as well as major cultural differences. When the McDonald's Corporation opened franchises in the Middle East, it responded to cultural differences by modifying the menus to reflect the dietary requirements of people who follow the Jewish and Muslim religions.

Fast-food restaurants are the most common type of franchise in the Middle East. Other potentially good industries include automotive service, clothing, printing centers, and travel agencies. The best potential for franchise development is in Israel, Egypt, Kuwait, Saudi Arabia, and the United Arab Emirates. Iran, Iraq, and Lebanon are not likely markets because of political instability and strong anti-U.S. sentiment.

Central and Eastern Europe

By the late 1990s the economy of many European countries that had operated under communism for forty years had stabilized after a ten-year transition to a capitalist system. Many people in the former Communist countries were used to shortages of products—and usually substandard products. Those people now want products and services that are of good quality and consistently available. Many Central and Eastern European residents now have discretionary income: They have extra money to spend on things they want but don't necessarily need.

Entrepreneurs in countries like Bulgaria, the Czech Republic, Hungary, Poland, Romania, and Russia are still adjusting to the idea of owning their own businesses. They often lack the ability to raise start-up money. Because of their backgrounds in the Communist economy, in which people were not encouraged to show initiative, the entrepreneurs may also lack the motivation and commitment needed to develop a franchise. As the people in these countries continue to grow in their understanding of free enterprise, franchising opportunities will skyrocket. The best opportunities will be in fast- food restaurants, laundry and dry-cleaning services, auto parts and services, professional training programs, book and music stores, and hotels and motels.

South America

Although franchising has been successful in some parts of South America, it exists in only a few parts of the continent. As in the rest of the world, fast-food businesses are prominent.

Many foreign investors begin their South American franchising efforts in Chile and Uruguay. Although neither country has a large population, both countries are friendly to foreign investors, and Chile has a fast-growing economy.

Brazil

The South American country with the most franchise companies—nearly 1,000—is Brazil. Most franchises are owned by Brazilians because, until 1995, the country permitted nearly no foreign investment. With a change in the laws and good economic growth, Brazil offers an opportunity for franchise development in the twenty-first century.

Argentina

Argentina is second, after Brazil, in number of franchises. With Brazil, Uruguay, and Paraguay, the country forms a trade bloc called Mercosur. Argentina offers easy access to markets in the other Mercosur countries and is a good market for foreign products and services.

Colombia

Colombia is third among South American countries in the number of franchise operations. There are, however, several drawbacks to franchise development in Colombia. There is a continuing threat of guerrilla and drug-related violence. In addition, the poverty rate is close to 40 percent, which means the market for products and services is limited.

Europe

Europeans in countries with a capitalist economy were among the first non-Americans to recognize that franchising is a good way of setting up a business and increasing its chances of survival. As more European countries are accepted into economic partnerships such as the European Union, franchise companies must continue to work with businesspeople who know the specific country in which each business is operated. The most important factor in foreign franchise development continues to be a willingness to adjust to and cooperate with national and regional customs.

The fifteen countries of the European Franchise Federation (EEF), which includes countries in Central and Eastern Europe, had about 3,300 franchise systems in the mid-1990s and created about one million jobs. The EEF, which was founded in 1972, encourages and influences franchising in Europe, promotes the European Code of Ethics, and represents the interests of franchising to economic organizations that include many European countries.

For more detailed information on franchise development in Europe, request a copy of the 1996 European Franchising Survey from the General Secretariat of the European Franchise Federation. To do this, contact John Thomas at the British Franchise Association by phoning 44-1491-410458 or 44-1491-578050, or by faxing your request to him at 44-1491-573517.

You may also contact the IFA (listed in the Appendix of this book) to request a copy of the March/April 1997 issue of *Franchising World*. The issue focuses on international franchising and includes advice from international franchising leaders.

15

Franchising in the Twenty-First Century

"Franchising is not just about hot dogs and hamburgers anymore," says Bob Vennell, president of Jani-King of Seattle. "I think in the next fifteen years, franchising will be in nearly every industry. There also will be co-branding, where people will operate more than one kind of franchise as their business." The pairing of Subway and Dunkin' Donuts in many locations is an example.

THE WAVE OF THE FUTURE

After more than a half-century of growth, franchising is not slowing down. As women continue to enter the workforce in increasing numbers, and a large percentage of the population grows older, the U.S. economy is becoming more service-oriented.

"Service industries will see incredible expansion," says IFA president Don DeBolt. "We'll see franchise companies in industries we never thought of. I think we'll see franchise companies that provide the service of repairing and maintaining water pipes and sewer pipes because many communities cannot afford to do this on their own. I believe more new franchises will develop when government services, such as water companies and sewage and waste treatment facilities, are operated by the private sector."

Nikki Sells, an Express Personnel Services franchisee, says that companies such as Karen Marshall's Computertots and a supply support service for women who have had mastectomies are examples of franchise opportunities that are "just exploding."

The demand for services such as home repair and remodeling, carpet cleaning, household furnishing, and various other maintenance and cleaning services will continue to increase. Business support services also have a high growth potential. They include accounting, mail processing, advertising services, package wrapping and shipping, personnel and temporary help services, and printing, copying services. Other franchises with good growth potential are automotive repairs and services such as quick-lube and tune-up, environmental services, hair salons, health aids and services, computer services, clothing, children's services, educational products and services, and telecommunications services.

A Diverse Future

Karen Marshall, president of Computertots and chair of IFA's Women's Franchise Network, predicts increasing opportunities for women and minorities.

"There will be more women and minorities because you can be whatever you are able to be and want to be," Marshall says. "Women bring strength to service-related businesses because they are good at building relationships. That is an absolutely critical part of developing a service-related business."

Business-to-Business Franchising

Business-to-business franchises will also grow. One example is Shred It, a Canadian company that provides highly secure paper-shredding services to businesses, in a truck that pulls up at the business, shreds documents, and then proceeds to the next shredding job.

When Your Home Is Your Office

In the '90s, many people began businesses at home. They saved the cost and time involved in commuting to an office and gained more flexibility and independence. Home-based franchises, especially service franchises, are part of the trend. Operating a franchise from home reduces overhead costs such as rent or lease expenses. If you want to operate a home-based franchise business, follow the advice in Section 2 of this book. In addition, check with your city, county, and state governments as to whether you will be allowed to run a business from your home. The answer may depend on what kind of business you want to operate. If you operate a travel agency or events-planning business, you conduct most of your business by phone, fax, and computer. Your neighbors are unlikely to be disturbed by your home-based franchise operation. If you produce and sell signs and banners at your home, you may have to convince your city council or county board that your business will not cause an inconvenience to your neighbors with production odors or customer traffic.

A Final Word on Franchising

Whenever an entrepreneur sets up a system, tests it, proves it, and meets FTC requirements, a new franchise is born. Franchising offers opportunities to people of all ages. Franchises are available in all price ranges. But no matter how franchising grows and changes, some things will stay the same. You must have high motivation and understand the reality of what it takes to run a business. If you fit this description and want to start your own business, you should consider franchising.

Glossary

business format franchising An arrangement by which a franchisee purchases a complete system of doing business.

disclosure document A document, required by the FTC, that provides information about a franchise company.

entrepreneur A person who organizes and directs a business undertaking, assuming the risk for the sake of profit.

Federal Trade Commission (FTC) The commission authorized by the U.S. Congress to regulate interstate trade, including the franchise industry.

franchise A legal contract or agreement between a franchisor and a franchisee. It permits the franchisor to grant certain rights and information about a business operation to an independent business owner, called a franchisee, in return for a fee and royalties.

franchise trade rule A law administered by the Federal Trade Commission (FTC) that requires franchisors to disclose pertinent information to potential buyers of the franchise.

franchise fee A one-time fee paid by the franchisee to the franchisor for use of the franchise business system, trademarks, management assistance, and other services.

franchisee A business owner who purchases a franchise from a franchisor and operates a business using the franchisor's name, product, business format, and other items.

franchisor The owner of a company, who lends his or her trademark or trade name and business system to one or more franchisees in exchange for a fee and royalties. The franchisor usually establishes the conditions under which a franchisee may operate but does not control the business nor own it financially. Also called a *franchise company.*

master franchisor An agent or extension of the franchise organization in a certain area, which provides the franchisor's services to franchisees.

prospectus A written description of a proposed or offered business enterprise.

royalty A continuing fee, usually a percentage of the gross revenue earned by the franchisee, which the franchisee pays to the franchisor.

trademark A distinctive name or symbol, registered with the U.S. Patent and Trademark Office, used to distinguish a particular product or service from others.

For More Information

International Franchise Association (IFA)
1350 New York Avenue, NW, Suite 900,
Washington, DC 20005-4709
Phone: (202) 628-8000
Fax: (202) 628-0812
E-mail: ifa@franchise.org
Web site: http://www.franchise.org

**For information about IFA programs and
activities, call the numbers listed below:**
Advertising rates and information for the *Franchise
Opportunities Guide:* (202) 628-0783
Franchising Expos: (888) 872-2677
Membership: (202) 662-0785
Public Relations: (202) 662-0770
Publications and Information: (202) 628-0771

American Franchisee Association (AFA)
53 West Jackson Boulevard, Suite 205
Chicago, IL 60604
Phone: (312) 431-0545
Fax: (312) 431-1132
E-mail: SKeziosAFA@aol.com
Web site: http://infonews.com/franchise/afa

Women in Franchising, Inc. (WIF)
53 West Jackson Boulevard, Suite 205
Chicago, IL 60604
Phone: (312) 431-1467

Fax: (312) 431-1469
E-mail: SKeziosWIF@aol.com
Web site: http://infonews.com/franchise/wif

**American Association of Franchisees and
   Dealers (AAFD)**
P.O. Box 81887
San Diego, CA 92138-1887
Phone: (800) 733-9858 or (619) 235-2556

Federal Trade Commission (FTC)
Division of Marketing Practices
Washington, DC 20580
Phone: (202) 326-3128

WEB SITES

U.S. Small Business Administration Franchise Report
http://www.franchise1.com/articles/sba

Checklist for comparison shopping for franchises
http://www.franchise1.com/articles/chklist.html

Small Business Administration Web site
http://www.sbaonline.sba.gov/workshops/franchises

American Bar Association Forum on Franchising
http://www.abanet.org

Be The Boss
http://www.betheboss.com

Franchise Doctor
http://www.franchisedoc.com

For Further Reading

BOOKS

Bond's Franchise Guide, published by Source Book
Publications, Oakland, CA, available for $29.95.
Phone: (800) 841-0873

Franchise Opportunities Guide, published semiannually
by the International Franchise Association, Washington, DC, available for $15 plus $6 shipping and
handling from IFA. Phone: (800) 543-1038; write:
IFA Publications, P.O. Box 1020, Sewickley, PA
15143, or e-mail: amy@franchise.org (The IFA has
numerous books, workbooks, audiocassettes and
videocassettes for sale. Request a free copy of the
Publications Catalog for a complete list.)

*Franchise Opportunities Handbook: A Complete Guide for
People Who Want to Start Their Own Franchise,* by
LaVerne L. Ludden, published by Park Avenue
Publications (an imprint of JIST Works, Inc.), Indi-
anapolis, IN, 1996, available for $16.95 from JIST
Work, Inc. Phone: (317) 264-3720, fax: (317) 264-
3709, or e-mail: JIST Works@AOL.com

MAGAZINES

Franchising World, $18 per year. Phone: (800) 543-1038.
Franchise Times, $35 per year. Phone: (800) 678-9595.

MAGAZINE AND NEWSPAPER ARTICLES

"Fast Track," *Business Start-Ups,* June 1998.

"Shop, Look & Listen," *Business Start-Ups,* May 1998.

"100 Top Low-Investment Franchises," *Business Start-Ups,* May 1998.

"Hit a Homerun With a Home-Based Franchise," *Opportunity,* May 1998.

"Self-Evaluation: Is Franchising for You?," *Opportunity,* April 1998.

"Homebased Franchise 200," *Business Start-Ups,* March 1998.

"New Franchises & Business Opportunities," *Business Start-Ups,* October 1997.

"Pop the Questions," *Business Start-Ups,* October 1997.

"Do You Want a Franchise? First Answer These 10 Questions," *Opportunity,* October 1997.

"Financing Your Franchise," *Business Start-Ups,* September 1997.

"50 Fastest-Growing Low-Investment Franchises," *Business Start-Ups,* August 1997.

"A Perfect Match," *Business Start-Ups,* July 1997.

"The Choice is Yours," *Business Start-Ups,* May 1997.

"Do You Have What It Takes to Be a Franchisee?, *Business Start-Ups,* May 1997.

"Have We Got a Deal for You," *SmartMoney,* April 1996.

Index